Quarterly Essay

CONTENTS

Quarterly Essay is published four times a year by Black Inc., an imprint of Schwartz Publishing Pty Ltd
Publisher: Morry Schwartz

ISBN 1 86395 394 9

Subscriptions (4 issues): $34.95 a year within Australia incl. GST (Institutional subs. $40). Outside Australia $70. Payment may be made by Mastercard, Visa or Bankcard, or by cheque made out to Schwartz Publishing. Payment includes postage and handling.

Correspondence and subscriptions should be addressed to the Editor at:
Black Inc.
Level 3, 167 Collins St
Melbourne VIC 3000
Australia
Phone: 61 3 9654 2000
Fax: 61 3 9654 2290
Email: quarterlyessay@blackincbooks.com

Editor: Peter Craven
Management: Silvia Kwon
Assistant Editor: Chris Feik
Publishing Assistant: Sophy Williams
Publicity: Meredith Kelly
Design: Guy Mirabella

AAP Image/Dean Lewis

Quarterly Essay aims to present significant contributions to political, intellectual and cultural debate. It is a magazine in extended pamphlet form and by publishing in each issue a single writer of at least 20,000 words we hope to mediate between the limitations of the newspaper column, where there is the danger that evidence and argument can be swallowed up by the form, and the kind of full-length study of a subject where the only readership is a necessarily specialised one. *Quarterly Essay* aims for the attention of the committed general reader. Although it is a periodical which wants subscribers, each number of the journal will be the length of a short book because we want our writers to have the opportunity to speak to the broadest possible audience without condescension or populist shortcuts. *Quarterly Essay* wants to get away from the tyranny that space limits impose in contemporary journalism and we will be giving our essayists the space to express the evidence for their views and those who disagree with them the chance to reply at whatever length is necessary. *Quarterly Essay* will not be confined to politics but it will be centrally concerned with it. We are not interested in occupying any particular point on the political map and we hope to bring our readership the widest range of political and cultural opinion which is compatible with truth-telling, style and command of the essay form.

INTRODUCTION

However hard it may be to be fair to our politicians, we cannot fail to be intensely aware of them. Guy Rundle's *The Opportunist* is an attempt to come to terms with John Howard at a time when the earth feels as if it has moved beneath our feet and his. A year or six months ago, there was the widespread feeling, among the public as well as the pundits, that John Howard's days as Prime Minister of Australia were almost certainly numbered – that despite the record of more or less sound economic management of the hardpnosed kind which he shared with his Labor predecessors, and despite the signal achievement of having gone to the people with a GST (a tax reform abhorrent to ordinary citizens but almost universally applauded by the governing classes), his government had lost credibility at a time when things continued to seem hard for the average person.

Now all that has changed. Refugee boats penetrating our waters and terrorists wreaking havoc on our great and powerful ally are godsends to John Howard, and Guy Rundle's *Quarterly Essay* is an attempt to find out why. This examination of something like the mind of John Howard began in opposite circumstances, as an almost elegiac look at how a man who had never had anything but a negative hold on the imaginations of the Australian intelligentsia could lead the government of a pluralised country beset with the heartbreaks and excitements that go along with a harsh environment of economic liberalism.

Rundle's John Howard essay retains this feature but has the added dramatic urgency of relating how recent events have shadowed everything but brightened John Howard's political prospects, as we stand on the knife edge of a November 10 election called at a moment's notice by the Prime Minister in order to maximise his advantage.

A significant minority of Australians think that John Howard (as well as Kim Beazley) behaved disgracefully over the *Tampa* refugees, and that the coincidence of the terrorist attacks on the World Trade Center and the Pentagon was the double whammy of an opportunity that only a man of unusual good fortune and unusual unscrupulousness could exploit. Guy Rundle's essay is an attempt to understand the kind of mind that could see political advantage in such pity and such terror.

It begins with the scandal of the treatment of the refugees and it ends with the toxic excitements of the terrorist attack and what a reasonable response might have been. Along the way we are invited to contemplate what it was about John Howard that made him the man of this moment, what it is that he stands for in terms of the mythology that sustains him, and what kind of dreaming of a national destiny or an essential Australian character this has involved for him.

Rundle is fascinated by the fact that John Howard is an economic liberal with a market-rules approach to the economy who is at the same time a social conservative who believes we can turn back the clock to the days of white picket fences in a monocultural world. He relates this socially regressive contradiction in John Howard to his deep affinity for the kind of battler ethos that surfaced in Pauline Hanson and, in turn, to the sort of nationalism that reared its head in Howard's constitutional preamble draft, with its implicit defiance of all those shameful black armbanders.

This is an essay by a man who is at least as much a social theorist as he is a political commentator, who wants to understand how John Howard's 'dreaming' relates to Menzies's cult of the 'forgotten people', on the one hand, and on the other, to the very different approaches to a mutating society of rather more up-to-date Liberals like Peter Costello and Jeff Kennett.

It is an attempt at an archeology of the legends that sustain a politician's vision and an attempt to uncover why it is that this 'mythology' is at once lacklustre and 'naive', even though, as Rundle notes in a fascinating aside which has implications for the kind of ideological narrative he traces, John Howard is, in various ways, more agnostic, more removed from his own sustaining beliefs than is usual in a politician.

Hence the parallel Rundle draws with Richard Nixon – not the overreaching and disreputable Nixon of Watergate, but the tricky character who would always take the current when it served, wherever it led him, in order to save his ventures.

The Opportunist is one of those fine crowded pieces of social analysis, written at a time of crisis, with an election looming like a nemesis, which is both an intellectual history of an unsympathetic politician and, at the margins, a denunciation of the opportunism he has displayed. It is an essay full of rich tensions and contradictions because Rundle, one of the most brilliant of the nation's younger thinkers on the Left, stands at the furthest possible remove from the world view John Howard so quietly and so confidently insinuates, yet he is mesmerised by the man's negative capability as someone might be by a snake. This is a very different Guy Rundle from the one who wrote the recent Max Gillies show about the Prime Minister (and presented him at one point as Barry Humphries's Sandy Stone) but it shows the same moodiness and eloquence and savage wit. Only Guy Rundle could bring together the limitations of John Howard's anti-drug campaign and the drek-stained lustre, black but glamour-laden, of a *liebestod* directed by Fassbinder.

One of Rundle's starting points, of which we can see the faint outlines, was that he was not (like so many people of his age or most members of the so-called élites of any age) offended by the Prime Minister's personal style. *The Opportunist* is among other things an attempt to understand the ways in which a vision shaped by the 'little person' mentality of suburban shopkeepers could allow John Howard to have such an empathy for what is most regressive and uncomprehending in the Australian tradition.

The Opportunist is the story, told through a suite of analytical musings, of how we have ended up with a prime minister who, while wearing the face of mildness and unassuming dignity, has at the eleventh hour recreated himself, presented himself anew as the thing he always was: the political leader in recent Australian history with the deepest affinity for

White Australia, One Nation, fear of the faceless hordes – the whole horror show that can be beaten up to transfix an electorate during a time of disquiet and appall.

So this essay is a portrait of a political opportunist who is also – though this is no excuse – a sincere reactionary: turning back the clock because he believes in it but also fanning the whirlwind of unreason in order to save his political skin.

Rundle's is a dazzling fragmented portrait, more like a de Kooning than a Lucian Freud, because the portraitist keeps having to retrieve himself from his own obsessive technical problems that threaten to swamp his sense of the subject, though it is retrieved with much greater vividness because of this tension. This is, among other things, a case of John Howard in the context of Brunswick St and Oxford St and of John Howard's sensibility brought eyeball-to-eyeball with a sensibility, at once mordant and self-involved, that cannot *believe* all this drivel about Family, Mateship and the bloody picket fence.

But it is also more than that, just as there is more to this *Quarterly Essay* than John Howard as an individual. Rundle is the kind of young thirties intellectual, as at home with the comedy show as he is with the intellectual exposition of ideas in the heavyweight journals, who is both exhilarated by the new globalised world of communication and appalled at what the new world economy is doing to the economies of desire, of simple human hope.

The Opportunist presents the spectre of a resurgent John Howard in this context and although Rundle has more time for some of Costello's directions, and more still for some of the Labor backroom boys, this pamphlet awards no prizes to politicians even when they have tried to look into the face of the challenging new globalised world with its high potential for individual tragedy.

Nor is this an essay which will give any joy to Kim Beazley. It is in the end an indictment of all those who will do any thing, betray any principle if it is expedient, in the quest to lead the nation.

Peter Craven

THE OPPORTUNIST

John Howard and the Triumph of Reaction

Guy Rundle

An Australian Coastwatch plane was the first to spot it, and it alerted the Indonesian coastal search-and-rescue service. A ship laden with refugees was sinking in the Indonesian sea, with an SOS painted on the roof. The Indonesian coastal service put out a general alert to ships in the area. The first to get there was the MV *Tampa*, a Norwegian container vessel making its way from Perth to Singapore. Its captain, Arne Rinnen, didn't hesitate to respond, nor would it have occurred to him not to – responding to stricken vessels, no matter how inconvenient it might be, was simply a customary law of the sea.

When over 400, mostly Afghan refugees were taken aboard the *Tampa* on 26 August, they were in an extremely agitated state. The Indonesian town of Merak was the closest port of call and Rinnen headed for that. Five of the refugees came onto the ship's bridge and behaved in what Rinnen called an 'intimidating manner'. They made clear their desire to go to Australia, and that they were desperate enough to begin throwing themselves overboard if they were to be taken back to Indonesia. Rinnen didn't want to call their bluff, and he didn't have enough crew to stop them if they carried out their threat, or resist them if they decided to take more aggressive action. He changed his course and made for Christmas Island.

When it became clear to coastal surveillance that the *Tampa* was heading for Australian waters, the information was quickly communicated to Canberra, where the Federal government swung into action. According to the testimony of Bill Farmer, permanent head of the Department of Immigration, under cross examination by Julian Burnside QC in the *habeas corpus* case pursued by Liberty Victoria and Vadarlis on behalf of the asylum seekers, the matter was almost immediately taken under the command of the Prime Minister and his advisors – rather than left in the hands of the Department of Immigration and Multicultural Affairs (DIMA).

The *Tampa* was refused permission to enter Australian waters and instructed to turn back to Indonesia. Captain Rinnen refused to leave, pointing out that the ship was no longer seaworthy, it had insufficient safety equipment for 500 people, and Christmas Island was now the nearest port. As the conversation of the nation – in streets, bars and across the airwaves – turned to the topic of asylum seekers, illegal or otherwise, the *Tampa* remained moored outside the twelve nautical-mile limit, requesting medical assistance. By now the 433 asylum seekers had been living on the sweltering deck and sleeping in empty containers for several days, and some were unconscious. Despite repeated requests for medical assistance, no help arrived and Rinnen decided to play it safe and take the ship into Australian territorial waters, at which point it was boarded by the Australian Special Air Service, the SAS.

By all accounts, Prime Minister John Howard was across the issue throughout – pumped with adrenalin, buoyed by the increasingly aggressive tone of talkback callers and tabloid media who had no time for the niceties of international Sea Law or refugee rights. Howard's firm belief that Australia's coast had to be 'defended' from such incursions coincided with an issue that could do him nothing but good in the heartlands. Opposition leader Kim Beazley had slunk to the microphone to endorse the government's stand in a terse and minimal manner that seemed to communicate the odiousness of the *realpolitik* decision he had made. The laws on boarding the vessel were open to multiple interpretation, to say the least. A Border Protection Bill was drawn up with mind-boggling haste and presented to the house. It was shoddy and draconian legislation which would have clashed with half a dozen other laws and international treaty obligations, and Howard might have been hoping it would be too much for the ALP to swallow. At this point it was; it went down in the Senate, and Howard had what is appropriately called 'clear blue water' between himself and his opponents. The general public could now easily see who was really committed to keeping out the queue jumpers.

'Those people will never set foot on Australian soil ... Never,' Howard said as he sprang into the press gallery at the height of the crisis. It was a line he repeated more than once on talkback. But behind the scenes he was a little less confident as he scrambled around to try and make a deal with anyone who would take them. As civil libertarians obtained an injunction preventing the removal of the *Tampa* and its unscheduled passengers from Australian territorial waters, Howard was trying New Zealand – a country the government had hitherto criticised for being a backdoor into Australia used by asylum seekers taking advantage of the Trans-Tasman agreement; and the United Nations – a body he and his government had frequently criticised for having the temerity to assume that its treaties could override national concerns. On the first morning of the Federal Court hearing to see if the *Tampa* asylum seekers had the right to *habeas corpus*, Commonwealth Solicitor-General David Bennett QC stood up in court and dramatically announced that a solution had been found that would make the entire hearing unnecessary – Nauru had agreed to accept the asylum seekers, numbering almost 300, above and beyond the

150 in family groups that New Zealand had volunteered to take. The last mention of Howard in connection with Nauru had been when he had declined to attend the South Pacific Forum held there in August 2001, sending instead his departing defence minister Peter Reith. Reith didn't have a great time – Australia was widely criticised by Pacific island nations threatened with extinction by rising sea levels for its failure to support the Kyoto accord and its blasé attitude to their most pressing concern: a guarantee of places for resettlement when the rising sea flowed into their fresh drinking water sources and made life unsustainable, something that could happen in less than 25 years time. But his stay was principally marred by the fact that Nauru had more or less collapsed as a viable state, due to financial mismanagement. Electricity was restricted to two hours a day and drinking water had to be flown in because there were insufficient foreign currency reserves to have the fresh water pump repaired. Reith's aides had to bring in Australian currency for the Australian journalists to pay their hotel bills because the local bank had no money.

For this and other reasons, the Federal Court hearing was not brought to a halt – because the applicants saw the Nauru option as something akin to latter-day transportation to a place that was unkindly referred to as a 'pile of bird poop in the middle of the ocean' throughout. As an agreement was reached whereby the *Tampa* people would begin a journey to Nauru on a navy frigate but would have their case considered as if they were still on the deck of the *Tampa*, the tabloids ran polls to see whether average readers wanted the 'civil libertarians' to continue their case or to cease and desist. The result was split along the same lines as might be the question, 'Would you like your children set on fire?'; and the court case was overwhelmingly condemned. Being arrayed against lawyers and courts didn't hurt the Prime Minister. Further polls found that John Howard's approval rating on the issue had soared to 77%, and that his overall approval rating was now at 57%, well above Beazley's. The latter's refusal to back the Border Protection Bill – a document that the normally pro-Coalition independent MP Peter Andren had said, in his refusal to support it, 'diminishes us all' – had given him the worst of both worlds. Liberal-minded ALP supporters were dismayed by the desperate electoral calculus, while those opposed to the refugees landing berated him for his failure to back the Prime Minister at this time of alleged crisis. Suffering from a persistent virus that he couldn't shake, Beazley sounded weak, hoarse and tired. Howard meanwhile had a spring in his step and was widely seen – à la the cover of the *Bulletin* – as 'Iron John'.

As he well knew, the *Tampa* was Howard's Falklands, a godsend. Had the refugees made it in on their original vessel, not even John Howard would have sent it back to sea – though a Prime Minister Hanson might have. Had Rinnen called the refugees' bluff and stayed on course for Indonesia, the public would barely have become aware of the situation. On the *Tampa* they were stuck but safe, albeit desperate. Howard's play was risky, but all indications were that he had nothing to lose anyway.

That the government's opportunity to get back in the game had come by way of the *Tampa* was almost too symbolic to be true. Six months earlier they had been all at sea and taking on water, with disastrous losses in Queensland, rural revolt, the revival of One Nation, and a leaked focus document declaring them to be 'mean, tricky and out-of-touch'. They bailed furiously, dismaying their broadsheet free-market supporters by blocking the takeover of Woodside Petroleum by Shell, and tampering with a fuel excise they had hitherto declared an inviolable feature of a non-distorted market. These moves got them up on the deck of the tanker, as it were, but the Northern Territory electoral result showed them to be becalmed once more. Though the unprecedented defeat of the Country Liberal Party had vindicated the Federal Liberal Party's decision to preference One Nation last, the cure was almost worse than the disease – the loss of the Territory had been as unimaginable as the defeat of the Kennett government two years earlier. It was a fresh reminder that dissatisfaction with the conservative side of politics had many sources, and that hitherto solid social groups could no longer be relied upon. Any one of a dozen forms of dissent had lodged in people's breasts, and it seemed that no amount of backtracking could move them. And then the ship came over the horizon ...

The overhead photo of that crowded deck would appear to have usurped all other images of the Howard era, pushing out other candidates – for example the sight of delegates to the 1997 Australian Reconciliation Convention turning their backs after the PM had refused to offer an apology for the 'stolen generations'; or the photo of him attending the Olympics with Juan Antonio Samaranch, with Howard identified only as an 'unnamed official'. It surmounts even the agreeably dowdy footage of him on his brisk morning constitutionals – the short-trousered boy-man striding through a series of foreign capitals like Tintin, trailed by bodyguards and camera crews bumping into each other's boom mikes. For those who support his courageous stand against the coming hordes on behalf of the battlers, the *Tampa* image summons up all they fear and hate about the erosion of an older Australia. The wandering winds of *Tampa* talkback blew into some very dark corners of the Australian psyche, and Howard's emphasis on our 'soil' and how he would prevent its contamination by Afghan feet fanned those winds. For those who thought that our ports and navies should honour the mutual consideration demanded by distress at sea, and that the 5,000 or so arrivals by sea did not present any sort of logistical problem, the image is one of enduring and actual shame. It was no more deserving of personal shame than was the revealed history of the stolen generations, but it was all the more visceral for being done in our name, now – that our leader had opted out of the most basic international civility, and that this would be attached to the notion of 'Australia' in the eyes of the world. Nor was it merely the so-called bleeding hearts who felt this way – even the *Wall Street Journal*, the newsletter of global capital, felt moved to call the decision 'callous'. Some of the most trenchant Australian criticism came from Greg Sheridan, the *Australian*'s foreign editor, who not only rounded on the cynicism of the *Tampa* manoeuvre, but also noted the most obvious sign that the overall refugee policy was actively dehumanising its enforcers – Immigration Minister

Philip Ruddock's disturbing use of the pronoun 'it' to refer to a six-year-old Iranian boy whose prolonged stay in the camps appears to have rendered him catatonic.

Each party had their own, more strategic reasons for taking such a stand, of course – Sheridan is an eager supporter of the Asian élites, dismayed by the reappearance of the rhetoric and practice of the White Australia Policy; the *Journal* was concerned as much about a breach of universal consent to the common Law of the Sea (and the attendant risk to the smooth flow of global trade) – but it was also clear that Howard's action had stirred up the residual political liberalism attached to their usually more visible economic liberalism.

That may be of concern to Howard after November 10 – should he progress to a third term, the *Tampa* crisis will hang around his neck as he wanders the world. But for now, stirring up a rare conjunction of the Left and Right of broadsheet opinion couldn't be better. It allows him to tap back into what has always been the mainspring of his political career, his improbably successful self-portrayal as a battler, a man who rejoices in the virtues of 'mateship', a representative of the average Aussie. It's a line he's been running since the early '80s, one picked up from U.S. neo-conservatives who claimed that a 'liberal élite' or 'new class' had supplanted supporters of the working class in the leadership of social democratic parties, despite a deep contempt for mainstream values. The disapproval of such people will do him no harm at all with the groups he believes it most necessary to win back – the small business battlers hurt by the introduction of the GST and the rural voters who believed that voting out the Keating government would put an end to the market-led destruction of a host of rural industries and communities. He seems to believe that he has already lost the significant minority whose commitment to social justice was sufficiently outraged by his government's policy on the Aborigines, the Republic and immigration detention – and they are hardly decisive anyway. Better to go in hard and summon up the worst side of the Australian spirit, forcing your more scrupulous opponents into a position where sooner or later they cannot bear to match you blow-for-blow, and are revealed to the public as the anti-patriotic time-servers they were all along.

The *Tampa* crisis may push Howard over the line for a third term – if the image sticks, and if more ships do not come over the horizon, ones less propitiously seaworthy than the *Tampa*. If it doesn't, it will neatly bookend the last phase of John Howard's political career, for the final stage of his zigzagging path to the Lodge began with a summoning up of the same debate in a way that broke the bipartisan convention that had persisted for two decades. It was 1988, and Howard's best shot at the top job seemed to involve laying into an ALP government still struggling with the monumental task of modernising the economy without making whole sections of the community redundant to requirements.

Howard was increasingly attracted by the socially conservative-economically liberal combination of the Thatcher–Reagan revolution. Having announced himself to be 'the most conservative leader the Liberal party has ever had', he did not wait long before ploughing into the issue of race, saying on the topic of the rate of Asian immigration:

> I wouldn't like to see it get greater … I do believe that in the eyes of some in the community it's too great, it would be in our imme-diate term interest and supportive of social cohesion if it were slowed down a little, so that the capacity of the community to absorb was greater.

The presentation of this idea – which had been first suggested by Howard's favourite historian Geoffrey Blainey at a dinner of the Warrnambool Rotary Club in 1984 – was craftily double-jointed, expressed in the manner of social engineering to avoid being tagged with the 'r' word. National Party Senator John Stone was happy to play the bad cop in all of this, telling the *7.30 Report* that 'Asian immigration has to be slowed. It is no use dancing around the bushes.' Howard went further in his repudiation of bipartisanship, coming out against 'multiculturalism'.

The move anticipated the *Tampa* manoeuvres 13 years later, with otherwise sympathetic major opinion makers aghast at the damage being done to the carefully constructed common policy by which political leaders on both sides of the House had been selling a certain vision of modern society – multicultural, global – to a far from convinced electorate.

The ludicrous Joh-for-Canberra push then put paid to Howard's ambitions – in conjunction with a widely expressed view that Howard did not have the personal qualities to be a strong leader. Nor could Howard make any ground on the 'common Aussie' image with Bob Hawke occupying centre-stage.

At the time, too, the reactionary culture of the shockjock and the headkicking U.K.-style tabloid was not nearly as well entrenched as it is now. Whether people were less racist than they are now remains to be seen, but the public sphere in which they could express such thoughts comfortably was less well developed. At the time it looked like Howard had made a terrible blunder.

In fact, it was a turning point in Australian political life, for it was a final assault against what remained of the 'left' wing of the Liberal Party, the small group who had found themselves christened, public-school style, the 'Wets'. This endangered and largely herbivorous species – Ian McPhee, Peter Baume, Steele Hall, to name the most visible – was all that remained of the 'social liberal' stream that had been a major – perhaps a key – element in the Liberal Party from its founding at the end of World War Two. The social groups they had appealed to had defected in turn to the Australia Party, the Whitlam ALP and then the Democrats, and they had lived on in the 1970s Liberal Party largely by the grace of Malcolm Fraser, who had given them some protection as political insurance, and because he shared some of their ideas. Those more attracted to the ideas of the New Right were determined to do them down.

The penultimate battle was over the ALP's Equal Opportunity Bill, much of it based on drafts and proposals floated by McPhee. Howard's wholesale rejection of it was a clear statement that any form of liberalism

with a critical position on society's capacity to steer itself towards freedom and equality of opportunity – a liberalism that believed 'choice'
could be defined as collectively choosing to change the framework within which individual choice takes place – no longer had a secure place in
the party, and that the social policy terrain would be carved up between
a small band of consistent liberals who believed in the primacy of the
social contract and conservatives who favoured the continuance of fixed
social roles. Hall voted with the government, Baume resigned from
shadow cabinet and McPhee – who was in Melbourne at his dentist at the
time of the vote – called to say he would have abstained if he had been
there, and that was the end of Liberal Party I. Liberal Party II was kicked
off by the repudiation of bipartisanship on immigration policy, a move
that got out of control and knocked Howard himself out of contention.
The return of Andrew Peacock – once the candidate of the Wets, now
fresh from playing Cinderella to Joh's fairy godmother – seemed like the
ultimate repudiation and caused Howard to make his one recorded
contribution to Australian political wit, the 'Lazarus with a triple bypass'
observation of his own leadership chances in the '90s.

In fact, it was the eventual making of him, because it was only in the
context of such a narrowed party that he could eventually succeed as
leader. The remaining stray Wets were seen off – Chris Puplick was
dumped to an unwinnable spot on the NSW Senate ticket in favour of
North Shore ice queen Bronwyn Bishop – and by the mid-1990s, the
party was consolidated to such a degree that the definition of Liberal
moderate now covered people such as Philip Ruddock. It was all a long
way from the Menzies Liberal Party, which had been founded by people
who are forgotten today – businessmen and ex-servicemen such as E.K.
White and M.H. Anderson, who did much of the groundwork and party-
building to create the organisation that is now widely believed to have
emerged fully formed from Sir Robert's brow. The idea of a Liberal party
that motivated them and – to a lesser degree – Menzies himself, was one
that distanced itself from its more narrowly defined predecessors such as

the United Australia Party. It was unashamedly a party of social reconstruction, sharing with Labor the idea that there was a thing out there called 'society' to be grasped and moulded; it merely differed about what was to be done with it. Admittedly, Menzies, the political street-fighter and prime mover of the Communist Party Dissolution Bill, has always got more credit than he deserves for being a genuine social liberal, but there was that element in the party he led. But Menzies the adept political fixer was not the Menzies of today's conservative mythologies, the ghostly embodiment of a pluralist centre-right party.

It is to this latter Menzies that John Howard swears fealty, and with whom he believes himself to be continuous. In pursuit of this link, Howard has described himself at various times as a liberal, a radical and a Burkean conservative. He argues that in attempting to fuse free-market economic liberalism with social conservatism he carries on the Menzies tradition.

In fact, he has been the disposer of it. The welcome departure of the Wets in 1988 gave Howard the sort of party he thought he really wanted – one much closer to Margaret Thatcher's Conservative Party. With it, he eventually won power as a burnt-out and distracted Paul Keating stumbled to his end in 1996 – Howard's victory was one practically no one could have failed to win. In five years he has pursued a virtually identical macroeconomic policy to that of his predecessor, while relentlessly hammering in an illusory picture of big-spending Labor. He has spoken incessantly of mateship, egalitarianism and unity while presiding over a widening of social divisions, both of outcome and opportunity. He has proclaimed the need for a unified and pluralist party of liberal-conservatives, while allowing a reactionary force to emerge to his right, laying waste to his Coalition partner in the process. He has alienated swathes of those liberal-minded high-income earners who might have been attracted to a pluralist party by dabbling with censorship, family boosterism and naive excursions into hard-wired citizenship such as the doomed preamble to the Constitution. He has held himself to be the champion of the 'battler' while introducing a tax that uniquely disadvantages small businesses in relation to large ones. He could have seized the moment – as, at crucial times, conservatives such as Nixon and Churchill did – to make an imaginative leap beyond the narrow confines of his own settled prejudices about race relations and the Republic.

In consequence of all of this, at the end of a sustained period of economic growth, and at a time when the Australian economy seems to be holding its head up rather better than comparable economies, he has brought his party to a point where only the bullying of a boatload of stateless people has allowed him the chance to retain power. In his era, his party has lost office in all but one State, and that is expected to fall as soon as its government goes to the people. It is a pretty stunning anti-achievement – less defeat from the jaws of victory than a political tracheotomy. He has retreated into his own ideology, his dream of Australia, forgetting – as Menzies would never have forgotten – that it was, in the last analysis, something for the punters. Like all conservative dreaming carried far enough, it has ended in reaction. That may yet save him. If it does, the Right will regroup and further transform itself. If, against the odds, the Liberals do go to the opposition benches, anything is possible, up to and including the greatest reconfiguration of conservative politics since the founding of the Liberal Party in 1944.

ONE NATION UNDER JOHN HOWARD

Most people who disagree with John Howard need to believe that he is a conservative through and through – that all his actions issue from a deeply parochial and deeply rooted set of beliefs about Australia and the world. For such opponents, he's the repository of everything there is to hate about conservatism – its pettiness, its self-satisfaction, its seeking of comfort and complacency at the expense of progress. It's good to have someone like that around – albeit not someone leading the country – whom one can look at occasionally and feel reassuringly progressive. Yet on the other side, even Howard's supporters are usually lukewarm about him. Unlike Keating or Hanson supporters, few of them see their leader as personally heroic or admirable – he's just the bloke they agree with who happens to be in the hot seat.

The truth of Howard's politics and personality is more complicated than both these views. He is, of course, personally a conservative in his beliefs, his tastes, his manner. Although he has made some appalling publicity blunders – visiting a primary school once he was photographed in a sandpit, pouring tea for small children from a toy pot – he has nevertheless been wise enough not to venture down the 'pop' road in the manner of some conservatives. He would never have been photographed at the funky Notting Hill Carnival – as William Hague was – wearing a baseball cap on backwards. He realised that Nelson Mandela was the only world leader who could meet the Spice Girls and come off enhanced from the encounter. His Where's Wally walkabouts notwithstanding, Howard has a vestigial sense of the dignity of the office combined with a restrained personal style.

Yet in matters of policy he's more flexible, a professional politician who can distance himself from his own personality and do whatever it takes to win. In 1987, taking advantage of the declining power of the Wets, and the seeming likelihood that the Reagan–Thatcher neo-conservative revolution would spread even deeper in Western society, he declared himself to be 'the most conservative leader the Liberal party has ever had' and – very improbably –'the Messiah of conservative politics'. Asked about it later he said, 'That was a phrase for the time.' Noted the questioner, 'It was six months ago, Mr Howard.'

The standard line is that he is part of the Australian Liberal tradition, which combines the best features of liberalism and conservatism. Claiming as his own the founding fathers of Federalism, Howard notes:

> They were what we would now describe as Liberals, embracing as they did both liberal and conservative philosophies.

At other times, he suggests that Liberalism succeeds by being a combination of conservatism and radicalism:

> One great virtue of Australian liberalism is its capacity to offer the blend of conservatism that is so clearly needed. The times demand that we hold fast to the values and institutions from our past which have served us well. They equally demand a willingness to repudiate those attitudes and practices which are holding us back.

On other matters, such as the Republic, he dives deeper into the blue, declaring himself to be:

> a Burkean conservative – if you have a system or an institution that works, then there's no need to examine changing it.

Yet at other times he veers towards a sort of economism, taking the most unconservative view that:

> The new Coalition government will have one unswerving, overriding, national goal: growth – real growth, sustainable growth.

Sometimes he attributes to liberalism values which are those of conservatism:

> At the heart of contemporary Australian liberalism are a set of values that have guided Australians for more than a century. We have always been a … people who regard the family as the central institution of our society.

In fact, this is a position that would strike most libertarian liberals as essentially illiberal in the manner in which it privileges one form of social arrangement over any other.

Ultimately his government has claimed to 'combine liberalism in economic policy with modern conservatism in social policy'. And it is this distinction that has formed the basis of Howard's argument and philosophy – that it is possible to take the economy and society as substantially separate spheres of life and apply one set of rules to one, and another set of rules to the other; to deal with them through wholly different philosophies and ideas of social being. Few actual politicians on the Right have argued this so explicitly or analytically. It was implicit in the policies of Reagan and Thatcher, of course, but they were far less inclined to address the matter in such an analytical manner. For Thatcher, it was a question of restoring 'Victorian values' – the neat fit between patriotism, a continent private life and self-enrichment in the freest possible market. Reagan's aids dabbled in philosophising, drawing on both U.S. neo-conservatism and British Americophiles like Paul Johnson to argue that the 1960s had confused the idea of liberty with licence, but Reagan himself retained his demeanour of holy innocence on such matters.

Yet a genuinely conservative approach to social life is one that upholds above all a belief in the lawful institutions of a society, and of honourable personal conduct. A genuinely liberal approach would be one that recognised the full legitimacy of the separation of powers and the importance of protecting the judicial and legislative arms. Time and time again John Howard has shown that he is willing to use the 'wiggle room' of his liberal-conservative position to pursue his deep objectives – the maintenance of his political career at almost any cost, and the enforcement of individual liberalism for labour and corporatism for capital. Nowhere was this more effectively demonstrated than in the handling of the Ansett crisis. Having clearly been willing to intervene in the transport market to shield Qantas from the full force of competition, the government then withdrew to the virtuous position of being 'above the market' when Ansett came to grief. The capital behind Qantas was protected by a government/big-business 'deal'; the employees of Ansett were left to fend for themselves on the sharp incline of the 'level' playing field.

When political defeat has threatened, John Howard has been willing to do damage to the political institutions he purports to have a respect for, and to cross over into the worst sort of reactionary populism. Howard is far more Nixonian – more distanced, as a politician, from his own personal political or moral beliefs – than either his opponents or his supporters would like to imagine.

Howard is a conservative and he is sometimes a liberal but, in ways he renders almost invisible, he is first and foremost a servant of the corporate world and its aim of extending itself into every corner of contemporary life. His conservatism is not so dearly held that it would override his commitment to the global market were the two to come into conflict, as they surely must do. But part of Howard's trick is to refuse to acknowledge that the two could ever come into conflict – or, even more enigmatically, that if they do, the state can enforce a conservative social order as a corrective to the social fraying caused by the market.

Desperate to cleave to the notion of a free market and to maintain the idea of a bounded and stable social order, Howard refuses to recognise that the former is now the principal enemy of the latter. In order to keep those two spheres of life separate – and his conception of life intact – Howard must pass from the actual to the imaginary, from a real encounter with a changing, dynamic society to the dream of one where it all fits together, without conflict, without contradiction. That he is also a thoroughly professional politician should not be lost sight of, however – Howard is no Jim Cairns of the Right. He knows how to talk plausibly and minimally of the necessity to balance forces within the field of social life. It is only when he feels that he is on firm ground that he lets the choke out and displays some of the more unusual features of his inner political life – a process nowhere more visible than in his championing of the doomed 'preamble' to the Constitution, a political moment to which I will return.

It is Howard's dreaming we have lived through for the past five years, and may yet live through for another five.

John Howard's Dreaming

A number of themes have persisted through Howard's political career in and out of government. The most prominent is unity. It is a theme to which he returns almost obsessively. As Australians, we are all one. The things that unite us are more important than the things that divide us. We are indivisible. He has been fortunate beyond belief that the most effective force promoting the feasibility of such false unities – attack from without – has occurred in the months leading up to the election. But like all good politicians, Howard is 'willing to be lucky' – neither the terrorist attack on America nor the arrival of the *Tampa* refugees were actual attacks from without on Australia. But Howard and his team span the message so effectively that it seemed to many people automatic and inevitable to believe that they were.

Yet Howard's unity is paradoxical, at least in a contemporary setting. It is a unity that has no need to be worked for, that does not require recognition of different interests, origins, affinities. It is not a unity that comes about through dialogue and an effort at mutual understanding; it is a unity that was always there, that is, as the conservative philosopher Roger Scruton would say, 'pre-political'. For Howard this unity – which is basically that of the Anglo-Celtic settler Australia, pre-multiculturalism – is something that can never be spoken about as a historical phenomenon, founded on conflict and contradiction, for to speak about it as such would be to acknowledge that it is historically determined, and therefore subject to change.

For this reason, Howard is extraordinarily hypersensitive to debate around the origins, histories and differences of contemporary Australia. Any attempt to discuss the degree to which Australia is a community constituted from diverse sources, who to some extent retain their differences, is taken to be an attack upon it. When interviewed on Four Corners in 1995 he said, famously, that he wanted Australians to feel more 'comfortable and relaxed' about their society – that is, free from anxiety, free from guilt, free from thinking about ourselves, from any kind of reflective self-scrutiny. To be comfortable and relaxed is to be unconscious of self, to not have to think about one's position in the universe.

Later, on his final long-awaited ascension to the prime ministership, he said that he hoped that one result of this was that people could now talk about things more openly, with less of a sense of guilt. It was both an acknowledgement that there had been a debate about identity and that such debate had now to be repressed if identity was to survive. The paradoxical logic was all-encompassing. It was necessary to speak of the way in which our society had come together, but by speaking of it one acknowledged that Australia's was a society of distinct elements. Consequently, debate about the nature of Australian society was inherently divisive – any suggestion that our core identity was less than an inviolable unity was an attack on that inviolable unity.

In service to this he adopted and hammered in endlessly the term 'political correctness', a concept imported from the U.S. in the early '90s by right-wing columnists such as P.P. McGuinness, who fought their own local versions of the U.S. culture wars in the broadsheets and later in journals such as Quadrant. 'Political correctness' was a usefully 'spectral' political force – its opponents brought it into being simply by mentioning it, conjuring up a nemesis they then sought to combat.

Circumstances soon gave Howard his chance to wage war on this nemesis. The High Court's 1992 Mabo decision and the subsequent Native Title Act had grounded indigenous claims in the common law, allowing conservative forces to align themselves not only against Aboriginal land rights, but against the entire judicial power. Keating's Redfern speech had conceded a historic responsibility that the conservative heartland were loathe to admit or – more sinisterly – even to see as involving wrong-doing, and Keating, the serial enthusiast *sine qua non*, had moved from economic zealotry to questions of national identity re-oriented around defining a less Anglo-Australian tradition and a new reorientation to Asia.

From the outset, Howard was determined to de-limit such debates in the most illiberal manner possible – by accusing his opponents of attempt-ing to stifle and censor discussion if they merely expressed divergent opinion. The debate around native title and myriad other issues through-out the early '90s was as vigorous, forthright and sometimes ill-tempered as debate in a genuinely liberal society is wont to be. By no fair assessment could it be said to be a debate in which there was an attempt to stifle discussion. Yet it was one of Howard's masterstrokes to make it look as if the silent majority were a 'silenced majority', despite the fact that centre-right voices continued to dominate the opinion pages of the paper, and far-right voices the world of shockjock talkback. In 1994, he claimed that:

> There seems to be a cult in Australia which has elevated certain issues to the designer-fashionable issues of the 1990s and if you dare say anything conventional on any of them you're a sexist, a racist, a misogynist, a this or that.

That Howard's bluff was never called on these things – or that he could manage to get away with it without looking ridiculous – was evidence that he was tapping into something felt within large swathes of the Anglo-Australian community. That something was a reaction to any sort of questioning of the triumphalist view of Australian history. It was the very reverse of faith in a liberal public sphere – criticism was held to be a form of censorship and repression, and the reaction revealed how fragile were the historical myths upon which many in the mainstream lived, and the lengths to which they were prepared to go to guard those myths against any sort of critical scrutiny.

Nor does it seem that he ever intended to back off from pushing the divisive agenda of cultural unity. He was never going to pursue the 'annihilate and then flatter' strategy of Malcolm Fraser, who supplanted Whitlam but then maintained many of his policies. No doubt he had barely suspected that he would have to deal with the Wik issue and the revelation that pastoral leases were open to native title claims – a situation that all parties believed had been put out of contention by the deal reached prior to the *Native Title Act*. The debate around the Coalition's subsequent ten-point plan – whose promulgation caused Noel Pearson to call the Coalition 'racist scum' – saw him bring out the 'politically correct' tag at virtually every interview.

But Howard's relentless determination to pursue his cultural agenda of invisible reunification was made clear by his one-man crusade to attach a preamble to the Constitution. With his colleagues barely able to hide their embarrassment, and with the great but erratic poet Les Murray in tow – an enormous Sancho Panza to Howard's midget Quixote – the two charged around the country at different times, communicating by payphone. This is what they came up with:

> With hope in god, the Commonwealth of Australia is constituted by the equal sovereignty of all its citizens.
>
> The Australian nation is woven together of people from many ancestries and arrivals. Our vast island continent has helped to shape the destiny of our Commonwealth and the spirit of its people.
>
> Since time immemorial our land has been inhabited by Aborigines and Torres Strait Islanders, who are honoured for their ancient and continuing cultures.
>
> In every generation immigrants have brought great enrichment to our nation's life.
>
> Australians are free to be proud of their country and heritage, free to realise themselves as individuals, and free to pursue their hopes and ideals. We value excellence as well as fairness, independence as dearly as mateship.
>
> Australia's democratic and federal system of government exists under law to preserve and protect all Australians in an equal dignity

which may never be infringed by prejudice or fashion or ideology
nor invoked against achievement.

In this spirit we, the Australian people, commit ourselves to this
Constitution.

The preamble is a prime example of the paradoxical nature of
Howard's conservatism. Genuinely organic societies – there is no such
thing, but some societies are closer to the fiction of one than others – do
not need written constitutions, for it is a measure of their 'embedded'
nature that a cultural framework is taken as read. Genuine conservatives
are suspicious of written constitutions because they have the same effect
on a society that a pre-nuptial agreement has on a marriage – the very
act of acknowledging the social union as a constructed and contracted
thing removes the necessarily unspoken quality that made it a deeply
meaningful union in the first place. And if there is one thing that conservatives hate more than a constitution, it is an American-style constitution,
with its declarations and sense of national purpose written down like a
corporate 'vision statement'. Nor is it something to which liberals are
unanimously attracted. For most liberals – and especially those like Hayek
from whom Howard's economic liberalism derives – any attempt to
define a national character is a chimera, and a dangerous one at that.
To suggest that national character is anything more than the sum total of
what happens to go on within a nation as the result of the innumerable
interactions of its individual citizens is to make a category error; it is a
futile attempt to find a real and enduring essence in the sum total of
things that people happen to do. For that type of liberalism, anything
more than a bare minimum agreement about the basic political institutions is a potential threat to freedom.

There is some indication that Howard was not unmindful of some of
this in the document that was eventually produced, and then resound-
ingly rejected by the people. Yet his preamble is a pure example of
Howard's dreaming. Crucial to it is a sense that some people are both
inside and outside the nation at the same time:

> Our vast island continent has helped to shape the destiny of our
> Commonwealth and the spirit of its people.

One spirit, yet:

> Since time immemorial our land has been inhabited by Aborigines
> and Torres Strait Islanders, who are honoured for their ancient and
> continuing cultures.

Surely if the people mentioned were part of our people, the sense of place
would be better expressed by the phrase 'the land' rather than 'our land'?
Compare the phrase: 'Our house was lived in for many years by a Swiss
family.' So whose house is it? Whose land is it? Are the original inhabitants
part of the nation that is 'woven together of people from many ancestries
and arrivals', or are they previous tenants? The original inhabitants are
'honoured for their ancient and continuing cultures'. But who is doing
the honouring and who is being honoured? Are the original inhabitants
honouring themselves – no, of course not, you can't honour yourself, it is
by definition done by others. So the preamble is speaking on behalf of a
group that honours another group. Their cultures continue, but they are
outside the nation.

Immigrants get the same treatment: they have brought great enrichment to our nation's life – rather than, for example, 'The Australian nation
is enriched by the different traditions of the many nations from which its
peoples have come.' Instead, the relationship between the nation and
immigrants – as opposed to transported convicts – is one of the gift, the
gift being by its very nature an exchange between separate parties.
Furthermore, the very word 'immigrants' sets up a shadow division
between one group of arrivals and another. Are all of us immigrants, as
Franklin Delano Roosevelt remarked? Or are we making a distinction
between arrivals? If we're not, then we are all immigrants. If so, then
whose nation is it that the immigrants have brought enrichment to?
If we're not all immigrants, then a division between one type of arrival

and another is established – later arrivals are 'immigrants' and somehow less essential.

The effect of this first part of the preamble is to 'include out' both indigenous people and later arrivals. The aim of the second part is to defend the nation that has been rhetorically established from the attacks upon it. It is here that the preamble becomes most characteristically Howardian:

> Australians are free to be proud of their country and heritage …

This is the strangest twist in the entire document, and surely one of the strangest ideas ever proposed for a foundational document. It seeks to enshrine something that, in a free society, is far too concrete and particular to be so enshrined. Although it looks like a statement of negative freedom – freedom from constraint – it is in fact an expression of positive freedom – freedom to override those elements of the world that limit one's expression of selfhood. (Yet such positive freedom, according to theorists of liberalism, is a philosophical error – one allegedly characteristic of movements such as Marxism and national socialism.) Howard's declaration is all too mindful of the forces of political correctness and the black armband school of history that would attempt to prevent us from enjoying our ability to be proud of our country and heritage. It speaks of an attempt to restrain other freedoms – the freedom to be critical of one's heritage, for example – in order to guarantee a purported right – to patriotism.

This begging of the question is echoed in the following paragraph:

> … to preserve and protect all Australians in an equal dignity which may never be infringed by prejudice or fashion or ideology nor invoked against achievement.

Reading this paragraph is like watching a tightrope walker attempt to stay balanced without realising that he or she is actually on a tightrope. It only looks crazy and erratic if you don't know the prevailing conditions. Given the invoking of 'fashion' and 'ideology', the 'prejudice' of which Howard speaks is both racial or religious bias *and* a so-called prejudice towards the past – hence a rush to judgement on our ambivalent history. Hovering in the background are historians pluralizing Australia's past and mourning it, slaves of fashion and ideology, envious of achievement.

Taken as a whole it is an absurd and embarrassing, a defensive and frightened document, all the more significant for being almost the only sustained expression of Howard's deep-seated feelings about this country. One looks in vain through his speeches and lectures for any sign of a personal spark, a moment when the individual destiny is joined to the general historical current, but his utterances tend to be homilies and statements of the obvious, so much greeting-card Liberalism. It is only in the preamble – a sort of treat that Howard seems to have promised himself as a reward for gaining power – that a truer expression of his beliefs about the nature of contemporary Australia comes out. Despite all superficial talk of a weaving together, the key metaphor is that of the 'core' and 'non-core', with the latter at war with the former.

John Howard's Forgotten People

It was his sense of making a stalwart defence of the silent and silenced majority – both the mainstream excluded from a politically correct media and the previous generations who could no longer speak – that made Howard so reluctant to wage war against Pauline Hanson and her One Nation Party for so long. Hanson had gained Liberal preselection and was subsequently thrown off the ticket when she told an interviewer that she would not represent Aboriginal Australians equally. But the ballots had already been printed and she went to the people still labelled as the party's choice. She attracted a range of both Liberal voters and a whole new tranche of voters who were looking for a quintessential outsider. If there were ever a candidate whose views were contrary to the spirit of the best of Howard's preamble – 'to preserve and protect all Australians in an equal dignity' – it was Hanson, with her race 'loyalty', her expressed view that she would not represent Aboriginal people.

Howard's refusal to tackle the One Nation phenomenon head on is famous now – a gaping absence in the 'liberal conservative' vision provoked in equal parts by electoral caution, Coalition cunning and insufficient revulsion at Hanson's rancorous lack of vision. It was left to a new-style liberal such as Jeff Kennett – a man with more than a touch of reaction to him, but no real trace of conservatism – to take the lead in firmly repudiating the Hanson image of a nation whose very identity and peace was under threat.

Furthermore Howard was even outflanked by his own colleagues in the traditionally more conservative National Party, with figures such as Ron Boswell and Bill O'Chee making more concerted efforts to fence the Hanson movement off (although one doesn't have to cherish any illusions about the spirit of the National Party or the social views of its individual members in noting this manoeuvre). Howard's notorious comment – perhaps the most extraordinary of his many comments – was that: 'I'm glad people are at least able to say these things without being accused of racism and bigotry.'

For Kennett, the repudiation of One Nation was a vital staging post on the way towards a new type of non-Labor politics, one in which community was genuinely apprehended as a work-in-progress under-taken by different ethnic groups – a community of no particular or specified character. For Howard, by contrast, what Hanson spoke of – when stripped of much of its distasteful rancour – was nothing other than what a genuine conservative would have to believe, in order to be worthy of the description.

In her now legendary maiden speech, Hanson quoted Paul Hasluck back to the newly elected Coalition on the priority of 'social' problems (which involve the social issues facing one united society) over 'racial' problems (which involve two distinct societies facing each other within a common territory). She then went on to say:

> To survive in peace and harmony, united and strong, we must have
> one nation, one people, one flag ... A truly multicultural country
> can never be strong or united.

The scattershot nature of Hanson's speech, its hurt, angry tone – like
many a reactionary demagogue, she succeeded by not disguising her own
hurt and humiliation, but instead transformed it into a living emblem
of the hurt purportedly felt by millions – gave it a repellent air, but the
content was simply an expression of what one kind of conservative has
to believe to be worthy of the name.

For the liberal, societies are based on contracts; for the radical, on the
working out of a holistic human plan. For the conservative, they arise
from deep-seated forms of unity that run beneath whatever political
disputes may arise. Because these understandings are, in conservative
philosopher Roger Scruton's terms, 'pre-political forms of unity', they
undergird any tensions that may arise from political differences within
society. They form the condition of possibility for political dialogue and
debate that can be conducted within a society that will not be torn apart
by them. The rancour and mean-spiritedness in Hanson's speech would
have been easy for Howard to reject; less easy to dismiss were the core
observations of racial and cultural homogeneity beneath it, since they
accorded with the view of an essential Australian character on which
Howard's values were grounded. They were observations that could not
only be described as 'conservative common sense' but – scarcely fifty
years ago – 'common sense' *tout court*.

It was the One in One Nation that drew Howard and Hanson together.
I have said that unity is one of Howard's obsessive themes, one to which
he returns with the obsessiveness of a man on a ledge telling himself not
to look down. This theme is stated in several ways:

> One of the greatest things about living in Australia is that we're
> essentially the same. We have a great egalitarian innocence.

There is that continuity, that golden thread of unity that hasn't changed.

It is imperative that we reach our conclusions in the context that we are one indivisible community of Australian people.

For Howard, this form of unity is sometimes held to be 'uniquely Australian', an expression of the pure Australian spirit. Furthermore, this pure Australian spirit is best manifested through an Australian political party that is itself above any form of sectoral community interest, namely the Liberal Party. For a country without 'class consciousness', the Liberal Party is the natural party of government. What space then for the other parties which have more explicit social or regional affiliations? Howard's repeated talk of indivisibility promulgates the fiction that contending factions – organised around intermediate institutions – are a new element in Australian society, and an accidental rather than an essential feature of it. A national history that is, like all national histories, one of alliances, conflicts, compromises, contracts and pacts, is wished away by an address to all Australians.

This is the continuation of a theme that Menzies developed when the Liberal Party was founded, that it was a party for the 'forgotten people', those who were being 'ground between the upper and nether millstone of a false class war'. Looking for a way to distance himself from the discredited business bias of the United Australia Party, Menzies needed to find a particular 'home' base that had a more general application. The answer was to reverse the usual historical relationship of class and party, and to derive the social agent from the realm of the political – to talk into being a class that he and his party would represent, the 'forgotten people'.

That is not to say that there were not people who felt 'forgotten' or hard done by, unrepresented by major social powers and institutions, before Menzies told them they were. But it was his masterstroke to represent them as a joint political group – and one created more from the matter of their feelings than by their external social role. These were groups described in other ways as the 'petit-bourgeoisie', the 'lower-middle classes' or the 'subjects of the empire'. Menzies spoke instead to their interiority, their individual feeling about their social predicament. It was a performance all the more extraordinary when set in its historical context – the middle of World War Two, when many other predicaments (that of Australian POWs, for example) had a greater claim on the attention of the Australian public.

The key thing about 'the forgotten people' is that potentially everyone can be a member – the rhetoric constitutes a particular class by appealing to a general experience. It works off the relation of the individual to modern life, since with the possible exception of Rupert Murdoch and Britney Spears practically everybody can feel 'forgotten', ignored, humiliated by mass modern life. The natural class base of the 'forgotten people' is the lower middle-class or petit-bourgeoisie, those small business people, independent tradespeople and underpaid professionals lacking the protection of trade unions and the more substantial financial clout of property ownership, but the rhetoric does not absolutely exclude anybody. Of course, the Liberal Party was also the party of big business and the professions, but the interesting thing is the others Menzies brought in to give his party credibility and breadth.

Talking this latter group into being was a political move that relied on the use of a relatively recent medium, the radio. Crucial to Menzies's invoking of a class that was not a class – a group of individuals who were caught in the cross-fire of a class war that was 'false' in the first place – was that its members retained their individuality, that they were not – initially at least – to be gathered together as a crowd. The 'forgotten people' were an imaginary people – they were all out there, all forgotten, but what brought them together, the spirit in which they were manifested, was the avuncular, susurrant voice of the great Ming on the radio.

Is it significant that John Howard has followed Menzies in employing radio as his preferred mode of interaction with the public? Talkback radio

– especially the shockjock version which has arisen in recent years – is a very different animal to the radio of the 1940s, but it has two features in common. Radio, unlike television or a public meeting, is a medium of the invisible voice, a voice that – should one's concentration wander – could almost appear to come from inside one's head, rather than from outside it. It is this principle that high profile shockjocks of the John Laws –'you know it makes sense' – variety work off, and it is a mode that Howard has tapped into more successfully than even Paul Keating. Speaking to the housebound, to people in their cars, workers on sites, the medium abolishes the distance between speaker and listener, and generates the feeling that someone is speaking their thoughts for them, saying what 'any right-thinking individual' would say. It is a force that feeds loneliness and which determines public expression. Who gets to speak and about what is expertly managed by show producers – which is not to say that conflict or debate are excluded, but that the terms of the debate have already been constituted with a certain slant.

Numerous commentators have noted the role that media play in the process of 'building' a nation; as Paul James has suggested, nations are 'abstract communities' in which millions of people who will never meet and who live in different face-to-face communities can nevertheless be made to feel a part of each other's lives. The rise of mass media has coincided with the decline of intermediate institutions – unions, congregations, associations – in and between which national debates were once thrashed out. Unlike intermediate institutions, mass media offer people the apparent possibility of both retaining their individuality and participating in the national community, with the airwaves as a sort of disembodied agora. This illusion is ideally suited to the liberal political message that we are both individual and indivisible, and is one of the reasons why it has become the mode that dominates the political imagination, even of those groups – such as the ALP – founded on varying principles.

In the end, though, all Howard's talk of indivisibility does is serve as a salve for wounds being opened. For it is a signal fact that in modern

Australian history, it has been the leaders of the Liberal Party – who have purported to unify all Australians – who have been the most willing to take the country into divisions that do damage to the political and institutional fabric while at the same time deploring the divisive and class-ridden nature of their opponents. Fraser's blocking of supply tested the machinery of government until the rivets started to pop, and only Whitlam's refusal to test the notion of the Governor-General's role as head of state guaranteed order. Menzies's Communist Party Dissolution Bill has been portrayed as a device targeted at a group of would-be violent revolutionaries when in fact it would have given the government wide powers to ban any organisations it judged to be 'fronts', and to pursue a wide-ranging witch-hunt against the Australian Left. And it has been John Howard and his government that have been most willing to ramrod division on both the cultural and political front. Like Enoch Powell in Britain, whose 1968 'rivers of blood' speech was ostensibly offered as a warning of impending racial conflict, but was in fact an incitement to a racist campaign, Howard's buying into the immigration debate in the late '80s was the warning of a stampede yelled at the top of the lungs, with a gunshot or two thrown in.

But this was as nothing compared to the actual violence the government would attempt to do to the law itself, the separation of powers and the process of law-making when the other shoe dropped and the *Tampa* sailed into view. The initial Border Protection Bill, which the government attempted to put through parliament after scarcely an afternoon's drafting, was not only draconian in the powers it gave the executive with regard to people entering territorial waters, it was a legislative mess, cutting across a whole range of existing civil and property law. Retrospective with regard to human conduct – a mockery of the very principle of law – it was a profound perversion of the separation of powers, a use of the legislative arm of the state as a rubber stamp to legitimise whatever action the executive had taken. That even the contemporary ALP would not wear it in its initial form must be taken as the smallest of mercies.

The Border Protection Bill was the expression of a profoundly cynical view of government and power, an illiberal vision of what the state could do to its own people, and to the institutions its party purported to respect. Yet such a contempt had been foreshadowed, all the more force-fully, in the active prosecution of the waterfront dispute earlier in the life of the government, and in its collaboration with Patrick Stevedores. A set-tlement in the conspiracy case meant that the proposition that the government had conspired against a section of its own population was never legally tested, nor was the degree to which Peter Reith consciously or otherwise misled parliament fully investigated.

That dispute acquired its extraordinarily divisive power from the fact that it seemed to be prosecuted at every social level – from the encour-agement of the National Farmers' Federation to take over a dock, to the alarming use of attack dogs to clear out workers, to the knowing wink given to Patrick's effort to use shell companies in an attempt to make legal restitution of workers' rights impossible.

This was partly the old reactionary technique of finding the 'enemy within' – accusing workers of 'industrial and economic treason' (a line used recently by Tony Abbott about the Australian Manufacturing Workers Union, while they were conducting a reasonable and orderly strike in the 'Manusafe' dispute). But in this case it was also a form of political brand-ing, since the ALP had been scarcely less insistent on the urgent need for restructuring on the waterfront. Hitherto, the non-Labor forces had been cagey about direct and bare-knuckle confrontation with trade unions (indeed more so than the ALP, who proved willing to use the army to discipline everyone from coal miners to pilots), and rare occasions of direct confrontation – the jailing of tramway union leader Clarrie O'Shea in 1969, and the subsequent general strike that secured his release – had reminded them of residual class loyalty lying beneath the surface of the decades-long Australian compromise around arbitration and awards. Now, however, the numerical and political decline of the industrial work-ing class and of working-class consciousness made such attacks more politically attractive to the non-Labor forces, and allowed them to attack the political institutions and practices of a liberal society – primarily the separation of powers and the integrity of parliament – in the name of economic individualism, and 'growth' conceived of as an end in itself. As we shall see, this sort of political warfare became increasingly necessary the more a bipartisan consensus came about on fundamental questions of the economy.

The Howard government has sought to distinguish itself from its opponents substantially on its economic record. It was helped in this by a
small improvement in economic indicators that took off in 1996 – much
too early for it to have been an effect of Coalition action. John Howard
and Peter Costello are not shy of claiming that they are the only party that
can deliver a leaner, more competitive Australia. In 1995, Howard said:

> Of all the issues I have been committed to over the last ten years,
> none has been more important, none has been more prominent
> than my absolute commitment to the need to free Australia's indus-
> trial relations system, to change our labour market practices.

Yet any glance at the figures indicates that the Howard economic agenda
has had almost nothing to do with such outcomes, except by maintaining a pre-established pattern. In fact, the economic performance of
Australia, as interpreted through the narrow models by which international institutions measure national success, shows a recent economic
history broken into clear periods – one slow rise in the 1980s, and a
more rapid one beginning after the recession of the early 1990s. The
graph of economic growth is a perfectly even upward trend of just under
4% per year since 1991; since 1992, inflation has stayed at around 2%,
with one slight lift in early 1996. Multifactor productivity grew evenly
at 1.1% throughout the '80s and 2% throughout the '90s. Profit share,
productivity growth and other key macroeconomic indicators have been
similarly consistent. The only exception to this is that average weekly
earnings began to lift in 1996. As John Edwards notes: 'The political
debate on the economy is unhelpful because neither of the two main
parties can make a sensible public analysis of the causes and consequences of success.' Was it the tough restructuring of the early '90s or
a longer term consequence of the deregulation of the '80s? Or was it
the global upswing of the '90s taking both efficient and inefficient

economies up with it? And so the theories go on. Looking at the graphs, a Martian would conclude that management of the Australian economy changed in the early 1990s and has been in the same hands ever since.

But of course this is not untrue. In 1991, the new Prime Minister Paul Keating (who had been a Treasurer of unprecedented power) decided to roll his sleeves up and get down to the major *perestroika* of the Australian economy from which he had allegedly been held back by Bob Hawke. Tariffs were the major target and they were substantially lowered. Competition and productivity became the new high-profile organising principles with the inauguration of the Hilmer inquiry, and these criteria have set the framework ever since, across both the Keating and Howard governments. This is hardly surprising. As globalisation continues apace, those who would manage a semi-peripheral economy still in a state of extensive modernisation must accept increasingly straitened prescriptions about how to handle things in relation to the rest of the world. Pointing to the irrational dogmas of the Gross Domestic Product and other measures is no good – they are manifest absurdities in which more powerful bodies believe, and we have to dance to the tune of such bodies, at least for the time being.

Such a situation has created the most significant – although, one suspects, temporary – political convergence in recent history. (This forms the background to what makes Labor's capitulation over the *Tampa* crisis so intolerable.) Now not only do the right-wing members of social democratic parties accept the goal of a lean and mean national economy, but so too do those from what used to be known as the Left, such as Lindsay Tanner. Howard and Costello try to raise the spectre of big-spending, bad-managing Labor, but it can't be sustained – which is one of the reasons why consistent economic growth is no longer rewarded with automatic electoral support. People know at some level that a common economic programme holds, regardless of who governs.

In fact, as Peter Botsman has pointed out, the Howard government cannot really be slated as a razor gang conservative government, with social services and other spending either keeping pace with Labor or actually expanding. Spending on areas such as social security has risen by an average 5% per year, and health by 7%, although of course this disguises the degree to which many of these disbursements – health and education especially – have been privatised. It has also left much of the slashing work to the States, which is part of the reason why State conservative governments have fallen like ninepins. Admittedly, the federal Coalition has cut corners on research and development funding – one explanation for Labor making such a fetish of Knowledge Nation – and we continue to lag well behind in OECD tables in this area. This is the trick perfected by the Thatcher government to achieve cheap, short-term budget cuts at the expense of long-term social and economic development – an appallingly cynical use of limited-term government and the historical and political amnesia of the voting public.

The ways by which the Coalition differentiates itself tend to be ideological or cultural, and even here Labor is often not far behind them (in out-Heroding Herod). So John Howard's government, distinguishing itself from Labor, has sought to launch an all-out attack on the role of trade unions within Australian life with the *Workplace Relations Act*. Certainly there are provisions within it that no Labor government would introduce, such as the limit on the right to strike, and secondary boycotts, but how much would Labor roll back if it came to power? Labor was already heading towards a total commitment to enterprise agreements when it lost government, which can seem inevitable in a diversified economy. In Britain, the Blair government has been notably reluctant to remove the anti-union legislation of the Thatcher era, with much of it remaining in place.

In secondary education, the Coalition government has altered the mode of funding non-government schools, shifting the assessment of need from the composition by student to the income level of the catchment area, which produces the anomaly that increased amounts of taxpayers money are going to places such as Melbourne Grammar. Ostensibly this is to assist the range of small private schools springing up in the new outer suburbs, and promote choice, the mantra of Education Minister David Kemp.

Perhaps for similar reasons, the Coalition has made a fetish of competition policy even where the application of the abstract notion of 'competition' is manifestly absurd – such as the management of air travel in the world's most sparsely populated country.

Yet nothing the Howard government has done in these areas – with the possible exception of education funding – really departs in principle from most of the things the Labor Party would do if it took power. Labor is now a social market party in the European manner, believing that the state should only fill the gap where the market is demonstrably inadequate. Labor may have proposals for altering the interaction between the welfare arm of the state and its 'clients' so that the emphasis falls on the state's role in facilitating community self-development – the so-called 'third way' – but such shifts tend to be concerned with policies pertaining to services, rather than with how the economy as a whole is to be managed.

Conservative Family Values

Family policy – economic, social and cultural – is the acid test of the liberal-conservative, because a genuine concern for the vitality of the family (however it is defined) means acknowledging the capacity of the market to wreak untold social damage if left to its own devices. Conversely, those most determined to hold on to a liberal-conservative 'dreaming' are those least likely to adopt a realistic policy on such matters. When globalisation and conservatism collide, conservatism often takes refuge in a nostalgia that would wish away contradiction and conflict.

Margaret Thatcher's famous quote is rarely produced in full – 'There is no such thing as society. There are individuals and there are families.' Her liberal-conservative vision, like John Howard's, is predicated on the idea of two spheres of life – the family, within which the interests of self and other are held, ideally, to be indivisible; and the market, where people relate as exchangers of commodities. There is no need to reflect on the fragile or ambivalent nature of the family because it is a naturally occurring phenomenon like the weather, and any difficulties you may have in keeping yours together within the context of a global market cannot be explained in social or economic terms. Any conflict of interests or motives can be transcended by the inherent virtue of family life. This myth was at the heart of the Liberals' notorious and much-derided 'Future Directions' policy of the 1980s, with its univocal image of a nuclear family behind a white picket fence.

The myth of a self-regulating society based around the stable and eternal single-income nuclear family has always been necessary to any sort of liberalism that is not a libertarianism. It is primarily a middle-class myth, since it obscures the large section of the working class obliged to run dual-income households out of economic necessity – and gains an added political spin by giving the middle class and higher-income working class (or the 'aspirationals', as they would be called today) a social group to distinguish themselves from. Furthermore, it conceals one of the defining features of capitalism – labour mobility, both the prevention of it (as in immigration controls) and, more importantly in this context, the compulsion to partake of it. The 'picket fence' mythology obscures the fact that the market, according to its needs, will always dictate the separation of wage earners from their dependents. The conservative myth that the family is a pre-social institution is used to buttress this – physical separation doesn't matter, because the heart cannot be divided.

It is therefore no paradox that contemporary Labor has been a more consistently pro-family party as far as actual deeds go. Because the labour movement was founded on the notion that society does not happen by accident, but is rather a product of complex political, economic and cultural interactions, it has been consistently more willing to recognise that the family is potentially the greatest casualty of the contradictions between society and the economy, and therefore to establish buffers against the economy's desire for a totally casualised workforce, with its mobility totally controlled.

In 1907, Justice Higgins 'Harvester' judgement in Melbourne set the tone by benchmarking the living wage at what was necessary for an average family to live in 'frugal comfort', independently of the willingness of the economy to pay it. The argument that this formed part of the 'Australian settlement' has been sometimes represented as an uncontested Australian consensus lasting over three-quarters of a century. This conceals the fact that it suffered repeated assault by non-Labor forces from the 1920s onwards, and only survived because the political captains of conservatism determined that it would be too risky to try to overthrow it. If the Gorton government's various innovations in family economic policy in the 1960s stole a march on an ALP still suspicious of anything seen to destabilise the solidity of full-time male employment, the ALP more than made up for it across the Whitlam and Hawke–Keating years with a range of more flexible policies on family funding and security. Under Hawke, an integrated set of family benefits was established.

The Howard government has made minor innovations in family policy, in part because it became clear that it was – and is – absolutely essential to 'bid' for the votes of families in marginal electorates in order to win and maintain power. But one of the most distinctive features of the Howard era has been the lack of comprehensive rethinking of the relationship between family, society and economy. Spending on childcare was reduced by more than $800 million in the first two budgets – most regressively through the freezing of the maximum level of childcare assistance at $115 a week. The principal effect of this, as Michelle Gunn has noted, has been that increased numbers of families have no option but to use unregulated childcare providers. As Patricia Apps points out, the concurrent tax credits to single income families (a near doubling of the tax-free threshold to $13,000) were presented as an evening up of an anomaly, when in fact they penalised working mothers twice over – because they had to pay for childcare from income being taxed at a higher rate than non-waged mothers.

This was the final form of what had long been Howard's obsession – income splitting, the family policy that isn't a family policy. The possibility of income splitting as a core plank of family policy was something that Howard talked up throughout the mid-'90s – a last-ditch refusal to acknowledge that the single-income family was henceforth to be only one possible family type among many, and far from the most numerous.

Political savvy has subsequently dictated that economic family policy should reflect, at least to a degree, the realities of contemporary social life – though neither major party has moved a sufficient distance to put in place a comprehensive series of policies that would fully acknowledge this. But if conservatives have to abandon the economic fiction of the self-maintaining family – given that families today are buttressed to an ever greater extent by a complex system of social benefits – they are nevertheless willing to retreat into the idea of the family as the key cultural bulwark and social form. In the post-'60s era, it was common for conservatives to portray Labor as potentially anti-family, especially in the 15 years or so when '60s-era critiques of the family were given some credence. With the retreat of all elements of the ALP from positions now seen to be modish, the family has become the common property of both sides of politics. Nevertheless, many in the non-Labor groups – and Howard in particular – have held onto an idea that the nuclear family is the only significant social group worth talking about, the only form of human connection – aside from patriotism – that can be seen as real.

This, as Thatcher's quote demonstrated, is the hallmark of a type of liberal who is deeply, almost unknowingly, determined by an idea of human beings as homo economicus, market man. It is the experience of the sort of people (including Howard's own family) that Menzies called out to – the 'forgotten people', gathered around small businesses, unable to enjoy the comfort and protection of working class organisations but excluded from the relative proximity to power of the bourgeoisie proper. Their form of economic enterprise – small businesses like the milk bar or the Howard family service station; and even the geographical form of Australian life – with its preponderance of detached houses in spread-out suburbs – is conducive to the idea that family is all that is real. It derives from a somewhat grim assessment of life, a clenching of the teeth and getting on with things in a self-reliant manner. (It is, in one way, the opposite of conservative, because it conflicts with the more expansive conservative idea that argues for a rich variety of institutions and inter-connections to bind people into social life and protect them from the risks of isolated individuality).

Family-centred societies in the capitalist mode are, Francis Fukuyama has argued, low on 'social capital' – residual human interconnectedness – and on the medium of social capital, trust. Consequently they tend to sentimentalise the family and to idealise family life, viewing it as the source of all possible meaning (aside from the nation) – in deliberate defiance of everything that can go wrong with families, as if Shakespeare had never written *King Lear* and Tennessee Williams had lived in vain. Some leading Liberals have sought to dissociate the party from this sort of exclusively family-oriented mythology. Jeff Kennett was keen to try and draw in sections of the community – gay groups, for example – who had an economic incentive to vote Liberal but continued to vote Labor because the ALP remained some sort of repository of liberal or progressive values. But Howard's improbable comeback in 1995 soon put the project of a revisionist and pluralist liberalism in conservative politics on hold, and allowed for an aggressive return to a more explicit and traditional 'familial' emphasis in key areas.

The paradoxes and consequences of that approach can be clearly seen in the Federal government anti-drugs campaign, which was run as an inter-linked series of TV ads and how-to booklets in the first half of 2001. Drugs have been an afflicting concern in recent years, which is why such diverse people as police commissioners, nuns and former vice-chancellors have advocated, for instance, safe injecting rooms. None of this is anti-family. It springs from an intense communitarian concern for the young who are alienated from their families, but it is a million miles from the Howard comfort zone. It is a problem for any government and Howard has taken a predictably hard line, but it is instructive to ponder (at least symbolically and as an example) the contradictions and complications of one case where he has attempted to deal with this most obvious source of family anxiety.

The government campaign followed a sharp rise in deaths from heroin overdose – deaths largely attributable to an influx of unusually pure heroin from the global market. At the same time, there was also a rise in the availability and popularity of party drugs such as ecstasy. Coinciding with debates about safe injecting rooms and relaxation of marijuana laws, it seemed clear to a lot of people that a more comprehensive and versatile policy on illicit drug use might be wise – another move that Kennett had attempted to make, although he was eventually stymied by the refusal of the National Party to co-operate. Unsurprisingly, Howard was not going to be a party to the consideration of any policy on drugs that countenanced safe injecting rooms, safe heroin trials, decriminalisation or the like. Yet the government's television campaign was a further step back from the more rational drug education campaigns we had become accustomed to, into the realm of 'reefer madness'-style propaganda. What was interesting were not only the assumptions the campaign made about the behaviour of the drug-taking young, but the lengths to which the campaign was willing to go to script social debate.

The first part of the campaign featured a couple of grungy scenes – a teenage girl in a dingy room prostituting herself for money to buy drugs, a boy being zipped up into a bodybag. The effect was stunningly counter-productive, the aesthetic values those of European art cinema. The dingy room, the naked bulb, the anonymous stranger and the girl in a red bra that was the brightest thing in the room – it was pure Fassbinder. The boy being zipped into the bodybag – accompanied by a voice-over of children saying what they wanted to be when they grew up – was pale, vulnerable, too good for this world, a *Trainspotting* version of Goethe's Young Werther, dead for his passion. Anyone who had any doubts that the path of drugs was dangerous, mysterious and charged with the air of sin and death would have had none after a viewing of those ads – they were practically a marketing campaign for the lifestyle, nihilistically conceived as a glamour trip.

Still more bizarre was the follow-up campaign in which we saw a couple of seconds of the first ad, which then pulled back to reveal a family watching the ad and discussing the dangers of drugs, which pulled back to reveal another family discussing the family discussing the first ad which then ... and so on in an eternal recession. The accompanying booklet emphasised the importance of talking things through with one's children and gave a sort of catechism that allowed people to deal with any smartarse questions their kids might come up with. The absence of screaming from both sides of the parent-child discussion of behavioural standards was an indication that the ads' vision of families was somewhat sanitised, but that was to be expected. (Satirical magazine *The Chaser* summed up a widespread scepticism with a laconic headline: 'Junkie gives up drugs after talking to parents'.) What was much more unusual was the emphasis that the ads put on training families to behave as families, as if they could no longer be trusted to perform that duty without prompting.

In the context of a post-'60s society in which values are more pluralist and fluid, real families could not be trusted to behave like the ideal family of the ads – because, after all, if they could be trusted, there wouldn't be this drugs problem in the first place. Thus the eternal regress of the second round of ads suggested a form of social discipline – people were not only being told about what to think about drugs, an attempt was being made to control the ways they actually spoke about them. There was an anti-drugs message – although the actual content (at least of the TV ads) was virtually zero – but more importantly, what was being sold was a set of values and a way of thinking about values.

The idealised social relationship between the family and the state was thus reversed: instead of the family being the ground of society upon which the state and the law rested, the family was reconstructed as an arm of the state, to whom was subcontracted the role of shaping the behaviour of the young, in a manner scripted by professionals.

While the details of the campaign were left to the ad agency, the focus on family was clearly at the government's insistence, and it was this clash between the government's imaginary world – where kids had an uncomplicatedly dutiful relationship to their parents' wisdom – and the real world the ads had to try to relate to, that produced such absurdity. In Victoria, around the same time, the Bracks government ran a campaign that was far more realistic in presenting the downside of drugs – marijuana leading to social isolation, the unpleasantness of post-ecstasy depression and so on. It was highly significant that parents were absent from the scenarios of these ads, so that the campaign acknowledged a key feature of contemporary life: the fact that teenagers are inclined to make ethical and social decisions with reference to their peer group, and the social world encompassing it. In contrast, by insisting on familial pieties, the federal campaign offered a black comic allegory of John Howard's incomprehension of the contemporary world.

Is this making a mountain out of a molehill? I think not. Howard's desire to control how people talk to their children, to hold stubbornly to the idealised familial doctrines of a bygone dispensation, is of a piece with his larger defensiveness. Having decided that the social and economic values that obtained at a certain time and in a certain context are ideal and eternal, conservatism attempts to re-establish these values with all the means at its disposal. Such an imperative can license an almost unlimited attack on the present institutions of society – and particularly upon minority groups within it – in the name of past cultures and meanings.

What then are the characteristic manoeuvres of the Howard era? An attack on the rule of law, on the separation of powers, a disdain for the judiciary, an ideological gloss on social and economic relations and, when all else fails, crude attempts at social engineering. These are the characteristic manoeuvres of what I'm calling conservative dreaming and they constitute the pathway by which parties of the Right pass from liberal-conservatism through conservative dreaming into reaction. They start with Mum and Dad, the kids and the picket fence, and they end up with Fortress Australia, in which everyone is encouraged to distrust the Muslim asylum seeker.

Costello-style Liberalism

It need not be so, even within the framework of conservative Liberal Party politics. The crystallisation of a ruby will change the course of a river, Borges once wrote, and nowhere has that been demonstrated more clearly than in the two terms to date of John Howard's prime ministership. Had Peter Costello not learnt from the momentous failure of Alexander Downer's brief, inglorious leadership and had he taken the party to government in 1996, we would have lived through a substantially different period: more sophisticated, more pluralist, at the edges more humane. Obviously it would have been virtually identical in macro-economic policy – as indeed a Beazley government would be – and I don't doubt that Costello would have been tough enough during the waterfront dispute. But on other issues – the Republic most visibly, but also the Aborigines, social services, and greater tolerance of different lifestyles – the Coalition and the country would have been taken in a different direction. Would the brother of Tim Costello have intercepted the refugees aboard the *Tampa* on the high seas? Would the *wunderkind* QC have fought the *habeas corpus* case, against black letter advice, and then have changed the law so there could be no appeal to the High Court? We at least have grounds to hope not. But what does that different direction amount to, and what might the contrast tell us about the distinctive character of the Howard years?

Costello's thinking about politics and society is most visible in his recent inaugural Henry Bolte lecture, in which he talked about the decline of neighbourly society, and the need for a revival of the spirit of volunteerism:

> Community is shared experience. These days when schools want to build a shared experience between their students, they take them out of their comfortable homes and throw them together on a camp to experience a bit of diversity. Going outside our homes to share an experience with the volunteer organisations of society is a big part of building community. We could revive the volunteer spirit in

Australia – we could revive all these non-government community organisations – if each of us were to spend one hour per week in volunteer activity.

Initial reactions to this lecture observed that Costello was merely softening the public up for a further fraying of the increasingly threadbare welfare safety net, with the possibility that such social functions might be contracted out to charity agencies, Clinton-style – or, Reagan–Thatcher-style, simply discontinued, and people left to rot until organisations of an ethical disposition had no alternative but to fill the gap. This response was probably politically astute – the name of the game continues to be collectivising the costs of contemporary life (you're all in this together) and individualising the benefits (here's your tax cut).

But I do not doubt that there was also more than a skerrick of genuine feeling in Costello's argument, though perhaps not enough will to get to the truth of the matter. His argument about volunteerism was one that came from U.S. communitarian thinking, where it has proved enormously successful, both as a way of rethinking traditional problems of freedom and welfare and also as a defence of conservatism. Robert D. Putnam's recent book *Bowling Alone* combines probably the most comprehensive statement on the 'community problem' with the latest solution. He elaborates the idea of 'social capital': society's shored-up amount of residual interconnection that it is spending but not replenishing as we move from an industrial society to an information-industrial one. The 'social capital' idea has met with such success that it has traversed Left and Right – Eva Cox, a former research colleague of Putnam's, uses it extensively in her work – and in turn put up barriers of its own to clear and analytical thinking.

The ostensible openness of Costello's thinking about volunteerism was all the more interesting given the occasion on which it was displayed – the Henry Bolte lecture. Can anyone imagine that pugnacious old turnip Henry Bolte airily considering the structural underpinning of society –

how it worked, how it failed, the micro-changes that would make it work better? For Bolte, and for almost anyone actively involved in politics before the 1970s, such fundamental self-questioning was out of the question – there was right and wrong, it was all of a piece, and there was no virtue on the side of the enemy. It's not that Bolte – or Calwell for that matter – wouldn't have thought about good and bad policy alternatives and the small changes that make big differences. But they would have thought in terms of political or economic action – whether by private authority or the state – on a thing called 'society' that had an inviolate and largely stable set of values. Costello's speech was addressed to the hypothetical outlines of society they would have taken as given – that people connect, that there are neighbourhoods, networks, friendships, associations, sociality.

The consensus among serious commentators on contemporary life is that such assumptions can no longer be made, and that one of the key problems facing societies and governments in the twenty-first century is the core process of social reproduction itself – how society keeps going, how it produces socialised persons capable of living meaningful and purposeful lives. Putnam's book extensively investigated the diminution of sociality in contemporary life – initially noted in the decline of associations and organisations, but found to embrace a more general decline in people's appetite for group or even dual activity, and a rise in the consumption of cultural products (videos, DVDs, CDs, pornography) that can be enjoyed in isolation. Other analysts, such as Richard Sennett, have argued that the rise of casualisation and temporary employment has created an unprecedented social fragility. Others point to jumps in crime rates and the increase in depression and other disorders as evidence of the disjunctive effects of the transition from an industrial to informational economy.

Costello-style liberalism seeks to make the shift from a relatively concrete set of social values to a more abstract approach to thinking about social life. Costello's approach is therefore one that most conservatives avoid like the plague, because abstracting from society as it is, in order to think about ways it could be reconstructed – or changed by a process of reflection – closes off the connecting passage between liberalism and conservatism, and reopens the one that runs between liberalism and radicalism. Genuine conservatism cleaves ultimately to the concrete – real historical traditions such as the monarchy and the flag should not be analysed too much lest they be emptied of their mysterious integrating content. To have to talk about the monarchy in abstract terms – as a social binding agent, personification of the state and so on – is to put yourself on the road to getting rid of it, because striving to believe in it is like trying to renew one's faith in the Easter Bunny through sheer power of the will. It can't be done without a warping of the whole intellect into an infantile condition.

Liberals such as Costello sometimes label their approach 'liberal conservatism' in order to appease the constituency covered by the National Party – who have largely seen through this and decamped anyway. But it is unmistakeably something other than what we have had in the past five years – a suggestion that the way society works is a topic for questioning, not the site of received wisdom.

Costello is keen to redefine the relationship between social and economic liberalism not out of any errant intellectual impulse, but because he realises the degree to which the Howard years have been a wasted opportunity in terms of building a new and comprehensively-embracing social coalition. The voters whom Howard has kept by acting on his own deep-seated beliefs overwhelmingly tilt towards the older end of the scale, to the narrowly Anglo-Celtic, to the non-urban. These are all, in terms of comparative influence, on a hiding to nothing. Over the next ten years, the numbers of these voters – whose self-understanding is framed by traditional conceptions such as 'working class', 'farmer' and so on – will decline. Nevertheless, Howard's aim is and always has been to fight a rearguard action on their behalf, without much thought as to how the party he uses to make that last stand will adapt itself to new conditions.

By contrast, Costello's aim – and one to which his political interests are attached – is to change the party from being a traditional right-wing party in post-World War Two mode to being a liberal party within a rapidly evolving context of globalisation – a reflective organisation defined more by the way it addresses social problems and their solutions than by the particular and concrete values it holds, and in that sense a party much closer to the Keating model of economic liberalism with an icing of social progressivism.

Should we feel a warm inner glow about this ostensible commitment to a new type of politics? Perhaps not, given that the first Liberal really to try this was Jeff Kennett. One doesn't doubt his commitment to a more liberal society on a range of matters from sexuality and soft drugs to social tolerance, but it's clear that the principal effect of such a political discourse was to create a smokescreen behind which an arguably anti-social programme – from gambling, to roads, education and urban planning – could be implemented.

Costello's main task is to win back the burgeoning groups – the inner urban, the middle-suburban service sector people, the minorities, including the gays, the ethnic communities and the children of immi-grants – that by and large remain part of the coalition that Whitlam and his associates put together in the 1960s. At that time, interests were clear-cut and overwhelmingly political – legalisation, liberalisation and cultural transformation cut across divergent economic interests. This coalition helped keep the ALP in power for a good part of a generation and con-strained the interregnum Fraser government to maintain and extend the Whitlamite liberal agenda.

But the success of such a coalition also planted the seeds of its failure. It has created an 'information' class who have started to assume a liberal politico-social sphere to such a degree that they can begin to think about their vote in economic terms once more. That such a coalition has not been wholly sundered is largely due to the political savvy of the ALP's leaders, and the comparative lack thereof (Fraser and Kennett excepted) of the non-Labor forces. It is the reason why – until the present, bizarre conjunction of political events, with piteous Muslim refugees and faceless Muslim terrorists providing a double bonus for John Howard – the Coalition was facing probable defeat in a period of continued prosperity, and why it has lost power in every State but one. There are simply many thousands of people earning salaries whose size would make it over-whelmingly in their interest to vote for the traditional party of low taxation, but who cannot – for politico-cultural reasons – even begin to consider voting for the Howard team. Admittedly, their life is made easier by a 'conservative' Labor Party that is hardly intent on bleeding them dry.

Any genuinely new take on politics has to acknowledge a dynamic connection between the economy and society. Neither major party has really begun to do this yet. The transition from industrial to a globalised society creates a crisis in social meaning because it opens out societies that were hitherto closed and bounded. For all pre-capitalist societies, closed systems – traditions, religions, obeisances, myths – provided the ways by which meaningful life and identity was maintained, and such systems could not be stood outside of. The opening out of these closed systems, into first national and then global markets and systems, throws the onus for creating frameworks of meaning onto individuals and groups. This new imperative led, in the nineteenth century, to the rise of voluntary associations, brotherhoods, dissenting churches – and also to the retrospective invention of traditions such as 'Merrie England', tradi-tional Christmas, and even the Myth of the Bush. This is the period in which conservatism as a political movement is founded – it is a fixative that attempts to preserve traditional authority as liberals attempt to shake the pillars of the temple beneath.

In any case, the uneasy balance between these two processes – tradi-tion and liberalism – was blown apart in the 1960s, when the information economy began to gather momentum, and the process of individualisation in an fractionalised market became so great that no middle-range authority – church, elders, family, neighbourhood – could be sustained without ever-increasing strain. New forms of socialisation appeared, particularly the subculture. In such a context, individuals have a greater capacity than ever to stand outside the given conditions of their birth and decide whether they'd like to try and change them, but they are also subject to unprecedented risk, because the meaning of their lives is not made with reference to enduring social structures. So-called post-modern conditions – boredom, depression, addiction, psychosomatic diseases, social exclusion – are to this society what black lung is to coalminers. They are what happen when people find no context, nothing on which they can grip.

Such conditions – which are still in the minority, though they won't be in a generation – prey even on the mind of those who escape them. As Hugh Mackay has noted, many people are happier than they have ever been, yet the condition that most preoccupies them is … youth suicide. Youth suicide – cashing in one's ticket to the universe – is seen, accu-rately, by many as a sign that something is wrong at the heart of our culture. People ponder it as an emblem of their own risk – that they will fall through the gossamer webs of the market – by means either objective (social redundancy) or subjective (existential collapse).

It is this social earthquake that rumbles under the political framework that has been inherited from an earlier period, and it is the reason why so many younger people feel that politics does not speak to them – because it speaks to a generation that stands behind them and is gone from the scene. These are conditions that cross the Left–Right boundary, since there is little difference between the sugar-cane farmer who must try to compete – impossibly – against the world, the steelworker asked to retrain as a supermarket storehand, the teenage depressive who is already being written off, and the one with no access to a fully funded education in the first place. Late conservatism of the Howardian kind cannot even begin to address their concerns – but nor can a reflective postmodern liberalism of the Costello variety (or indeed, the Beazley variety), unless it can acknow-ledge that the desocialising effects of the market must be addressed.

The ALP is currently divided on the question of these social changes. The 'realists' are gathered around the leadership, and have in effect taken the party back to an era prior to that of Whitlam, and to a position in some ways less liberal even than that of Evatt's party. Another group – loosely defined as enthusiasts of the 'third way' and including figures who are nominally of the Right such as Mark Latham and nominally of the Left such as Lindsay Tanner – are looking to reinvent the Labor Party as a 'new' or 'post'-labour party in which all policy issues are taken as social problems to be solved in the abstract, rather than used to advance the interests of any given set of social groups or classes. Much of this thinking is highly creative, and can demonstrate more of a policy inventiveness than Costello's low-church gloss on the problems of social cohesion, yet it is also at times hopelessly Pollyanna-ish. Take Latham on the new economy:

> Hierarchies hoard knowledge and authority at the top of the administrative pecking order ... Networks, by contrast, flatten the pecking order and build up collaborative relationships. In terms of organisational practice, they are the antithesis of hierarchies. The wide spread of information in our society means it can no longer be hoarded at the top of an organisation. It needs to be dispersed and thus open up new opportunities for the devolution of power.

Anyone who believes that technological change will solve of itself the age-old problems of social power and social justice should talk to a Microsoft employee. Or one of its competitors. More fundamentally, neither Left nor Right is willing to acknowledge the utterly ambiguous character of transformational conditions at a time of so-called 'post-modernity' – that postmodernity takes away with one hand what it gives with the other. The freedom to be a self-defining person also involves the stress of having to define oneself and to make one's way in an increasingly atomised world. This ambivalence is keenly felt, yet neither mainstream political party has had the wit to highlight it as the deep structure of a host of seemingly disparate social problems – from the

gradual evaporation of traditional work and the work cultures that supported it to the multitudinous social and psychological dilemmas of
those who may be more fortunate in material terms.

The disjuncture can be seen in events such as the Ansett collapse, and
in the lack of fit between the structural policies that have been taken up
by both parties – relentless 'creatively destructive' competition – and the
humane culture of work that has developed in Australia through the
twentieth century: the idea that if you work conscientiously and loyally,
you will get commensurate consideration from your employer. It is the
founding myth on which capitalism depends; it is what encourages
people to do good work, to invest their job with meaning and pride
beyond gaining a wage. But in a postmodern economy, the degree of
fluidity in some economic sectors – especially the old industrial concerns
– and the relentless merging and monopolisation in other sectors, strips
the veil of ideology from work and profit.

Piers Akerman, the editor of the Sydney *Telegraph*, advanced the idea that
Ansett had failed because Qantas staff had 'worked harder'. Does anyone
really believe this sort of smug fiction anymore? Did Qantas stewards
push the meal trolleys down the aisles faster than their competitors and
thus enhance their employers' profits? Or is it that the individual's hopes
for a working life are exposed to an unprecedented degree of risk and
uncertainty in the new economy?

'Third way' thinking has relatively realistic ways of thinking about this
sort of problem, though it is committed to an acceptance of risk, fluidity, ceaseless retraining and self-redefinition as inevitable features of
contemporary social life. The idea that an economy and a society moving
at such unprecedented velocity may be uniquely unsatisfying to our
deepest human needs – for stable frameworks of meaning and living a life
– is something it is unwilling to address.

Costello's communitarian position has no way to deal with this need
other than through a secular sermon: 'Thou shalt volunteer ...' That the
economic changes he so vociferously promotes may create a need for

community but reduce the ability to achieve it – in a social context where atomised individualism increasingly makes sense – is beyond his ken, and he shows no anxiety to confront this.

Howard's social conservatism does address these issues, but the address is a false one. His positions take the content of previous ways of life – the flag, the monarchy, the triumphalist history – and imagine that they can be re-established in a new social form, in which the rich collision of such factors as the '60s revolution, multiculturalism and the new media can be wished away or somehow overcome. Such nostalgic conservatism is actually a postmodern sort of thing. It springs from the naive belief that symbols and artefacts can retain their meaning in any context – it is not a million miles from the 'New Age' belief that the rich social meaning of other cultures can be accessed through the recreational use of healing crystals and shamanic religious objects, or that a stable masculinity can be obtained by drum making and weekend sweat lodge retreats. It is an expression of a profound desire not to confront the problems that really face us as we move into a substantially changed world.

ANTI-VISION

That is somewhere along the road to capturing what many people feel about the Howard years. Until the twin crises of the *Tampa* and the attack on the World Trade Center, the Howard team had provided government that had pleased almost no one, excepting the CEOs of large businesses – scarcely a commanding social coalition, nor a group usually famed for the breadth of their cultural or historical vision. It has always been a *pro tempore* government, even for its supporters. Howard has never had the yokel charm of a Bjelke-Petersen or the cowboy élan of a Kennett, and any chance he might have had to be seen as the pugnacious defender of the 'real' Australia vanished when he kicked off his prime ministership by tackling the gun laws – a campaign that remains the sole act of pure courage in an otherwise blemished record. (If he rose to the occasion of the crisis in East Timor, he also helped create it.) Robert Manne has recently called his record of the past half-decade 'the barren years'; and Donald Horne has described it as a period in which we were 'looking for leadership'.

Until the recent horrifying opportunism of what Howard made of the *Tampa* incident (and the way the attack on America played into his hands), there was no feeling of a powerful or countervailing force to which one either cleaves or defines oneself against. The Howard years have been a fidgety period – dissatisfying, irritating, exasperating. Living in the absence of any clear vision, except to go on and to procrastinate, one feels that absence greatly, as the reverse of any vision. While someone with a vision tends to project out of themselves towards the country as a whole, an anti-vision draws people into their private obsessions and compromises. For a long time, Howard seemed to get a certain glee out of the systematic lowering of other's expectations, of establishing that there was less to things than met the eye.

In 1995, Howard defined himself against Keating with the idea that mainstream Australia should be more 'comfortable and relaxed' about itself, an idea of government not as leadership, but as stewardship – that the governor, the ship's pilot, has no influence on where the ship of state is going, but merely plots a course according to the needs of the passengers. It is an eminently conservative idea of government and a patently false one in a period such as ours in which society presents itself as a series of questions rather than answers. The interaction of expert cultures, mass media, the governing of a complex society and the multifarious opinions of interest groups means that there is no 'general will' that a leader can simply read off and enact. Values, ideas, priorities emerge from the interaction of these different social agents, and the leader who refuses to play a proactive part in this process is not creditably refusing to impose upon a sovereign people – he is leaving the ship to wander rudderless on the high seas of current possibility.

As Keating himself recently pointed out in relation to Howard's record, leadership is not merely about the knee-jerk reaction to immediate crises – it is about opening up the best possibilities of a society rather than the worst, over a period of time. For Keating, Howard's legacy – as reflected in the twinning of the terrorist attack on America and the *Tampa* crisis – has been to bring out the worst side of the Australian people, to flatter its residual strains of superstitious xenophobia by representing them as a commitment to fairness – the fairness of denying special treatment to 'queue jumpers'. It is leadership that takes people to the worst place they could end up – in Keating's terms, to a place where security is seen as being protection 'from Asia' rather than 'in Asia'.

It is, in short, the essence of reaction rather than conservatism; it is the understated voice that speaks to what is most base in the voter, and in manufacturing a crisis whispers the rhetoric of scapegoats, of enemies, of aliens. It offers in politics what cannot be achieved in social life – a freedom from complexity, from difficulty.

We finally have a prime minister who is virtually at one with the emotional priorities of One Nation. According to the polls, he is carrying a large number of the Australian people with him. But he was always in his quiet way a reactionary, as I have sought to show by looking at his 'dreaming'. Now circumstance has delivered him his finest hour, which to thinking Australians of every political persuasion is looking like one of our darker moments. It is a moment of opportunism, unrelieved by an abject Labor Opposition. It shows a ruthless political mastery, which is surprising in John Howard, but the mythology he is manipulating should come as no surprise.

The New Settlement

In the face of such reactionary opportunism, it's harder to say – though still necessary – that there is a new Australian settlement to be made, and it is yet to be made. You can see the beginnings of it in a hundred places. It was foreshadowed in the Whitlam years and it is coming to pass by the sheer force of demographics. It is inherently republican, if a republic means nothing more than that people decide how they will live and get along together, retaining such aspects of the past as they wish and discarding what they no longer want. It is inherently multicultural, because the world is now, and a 'real' Australian society has no place for nostalgic dreaming about the past in its search for a way in which people can live with each other. It will be an information-industrial society, an urban society, a pluralist society.

The shrinking populace of rural Australia are a welcome part of it, but if they continue to insist on their cultural primacy they will wither on the vine and few will care. We live in a country where cattle runs are the size of Wales. Ultimately, however regrettably, agri-business does not require the support of actual communities, and if rural Australia does not come to terms with the new urban, coastal society it faces, it will die and die unmourned and the occasional One Nation senator will not make much of a difference. Geography lies. There are more people in one slice of Sydney suburbia – lawyers, programmers, call-centre operatives, panel beaters, futures traders, supermarket attendants, you name it – than in the whole of the northern half of Western Australia, and they are more prosperous and necessary to the export economy with it. Traditional white

Anglo-Celtic rural Australia will have to accept its ultimate destiny – as one group among many – and any appeal to history or tradition will fall on deaf if not hostile ears.

There is a sadness in that fact, just as there is a sadness in the fate of all the Aussie battlers left stranded by a globalised world, but John Howard's clairvoyance about these people – evident in his caution about the rise of One Nation – though it is born of genuine sympathy, does not change the fact that he is as much an agent of their destruction as Keating was. His economics (which are the dominant economics of the world) will see them fall like so many gum-leaves. His mistake in the face of History – which may well be his short-term political triumph – is to imagine he can preserve the dreaming of old Australia by enshrining their values, by marshalling the prejudices that he shares with them.

Of course there are different dreams born of different possibilities. Like America, we are a hybrid society, a patchwork nation. Unlike the U.S. we have no imperial baggage, no momentous history to live up to, no revolution, no Civil War, no imperial command of the world. We're a place where people have come for a hundred different reasons, a place with a sorry past (the horrors of convictism, the destruction and ravaging of the Aborigines), but the possibility of an honourable future. It is the very ordinariness and contingency of our national existence that makes anything possible, the fact that we have no national destiny except to get along together and pursue our individual lives. Manning Clark mourned 'the kingdom of nothingness' that Australian materialism could become. But in fact we are the republic of possibility, the place where anything can happen, where everything is up for grabs. No one depends on us, except ourselves, no one is watching us, except ourselves, and that is the definition of freedom.

Sixty years ago we were a society where Catholics – who were called 'Romans' – had a healthy awareness of their difference from the Protestants – who were sometimes called British. Since then we have taken in more than 200 nations and there have been no race riots, no suburban wars between Serb and Croat, Greek and Turk, no substantial restagings of old battles in a new land. The racism that does exist – and now with the help of an unscrupulous prime minister and an abject leader of the opposition, seems dominant in relation to the refugees – is more like a recurrent 'flu than any sort of serious complaint. The next 20 years here will see a coming to terms with people from the rest of the world which no one hitherto would have imagined possible. When the *Tampa* appeared on the horizon and Howard did his pseudo-Churchill act, he met with 75% approval. Given the passage of time, that attitude will vanish as anything but a shameful memory; it will be as gone and unimaginable as the sectarian debates of the first half of the century. It's like the way we all now know that R.M. Williams is fancy dress – the only people who don't know it are the people who wear R.M. Williams.

The conservative vision of society as it is articulated by the reactionary John Howard is one which says, above all, that people cannot come to terms with, they cannot rise above their given differences and discover a common humanity.

What the *Tampa* crisis and its aftermath revealed was what many had suspected about John Howard – that ultimately he was an opportunist like Richard Nixon, that he would seize any chance he had to hang on to power. Entrusted with the task of guarding parliamentary democracy, he has first distorted it, then abrogated it, drawing the legislative function into increasingly disreputable action where, for instance, it can offend the conscience of the ramshackle government of Nauru or seek to deny boat-people the possibility of ever gaining full citizenship, even when their refugee status is confirmed.

AFTERWORD

On Tuesday, 11 September, when an earlier version of this essay was seven-eighths finished, I was shutting up shop for the day, unwinding by watching *The West Wing*, the midcult soap-opera choice of politics junkies everywhere. I looked away and when I came back there was a shot of a plane ploughing into the World Trade Center and exploding. The momentary illusion that this was part of the story gave way to the realisation that has now been ceaselessly commented upon – that a rupture had occurred in the historico-political fabric, and we had now in an instant been flung into a new era. During the subsequent coverage relayed from U.S. networks, it was clear that the smooth functioning of the global media society had been as effectively exploded as those now-vanished skyscrapers – network anchors were flustered, information was incomplete, the realisation that the Pentagon had been hit took a while to sink in, the uplinks fell away, cell phones didn't work, all bets were off.

It was a peek behind the scenes of the complex web of contemporary life and power, and a chastening glimpse of how fragile it all was. But from home still worse was to come.

The intersecting events of the asylum seeker debate-cum-farce were gazumped comprehensively by the events in America, the horror of that event, and the scarcely less frightening reaction on the part of American commentators and large sections of its general public. Even by the second day out from the tragedy, things were moving very fast, and President George W. Bush had announced that the United States was at war. That it wasn't at war by any hitherto agreed-upon definition of an act of war – the terrorist attack was still a criminal act, albeit one of immense destructiveness – scarcely seemed to matter in the rush to mobilisation. It was a mobilisation that inevitably took in Australia too, with the Howard government offering the U.S. government a 'blank cheque' of support – together with the ever-obedient United Kingdom, the nation most unquestioningly acquiescent to a U.S.-led war on terrorism.

Futile as it is to do so, it needs to be pointed out that there was no obligation under our treaties to offer such unquestioning support or to promise that our support would continue to be unquestioning. A genuinely prudent leader, with the interests of his own people at heart, would have taken particular American actions on a case-by-case basis, within a framework of in-principle support. It was by such an act – John Curtin's refusal to give Winston Churchill a blank cheque of support in World War Two – that our alliance with the U.S. was made, in the name of Australian interests having primacy over that of the Empire. That leaves us under no obligation to stay signed up to the new empire, nor are our best interests or our security served by being seen to be indistinguishable from it.

Throughout his career, John Howard has talked of unity and sowed division, splitting off sections of society that can be demonised as the other in the name of the pure whole. He has cut with the grain of the worst in us and pushed One Nation to the margins by taking on its spirit.

The coincident occurrence of the asylum seeker confrontation and the attack on the U.S. has made visible the most dangerous and damaging thing he has done to the Australian polity – aided by the shockjocks and ratbag columnists – and that is to deepen contempt for such protection as we did have from unbridled executive power, mass hysteria, the rush to surrender our freedoms and offer them up on the altar of crisis. Now we have a situation in which our dominant 'ally' has moved into a mode of threatening belligerence – a state in which the greatest injury is perceived not to be the suffering inflicted on the populace but the affront made to American 'strength' and 'greatness' – at the same time as our approach to refugees sailed into the waters of barbarity.

A good governor of whatever stripe would have looked ahead, would have seen the dangers implicit in setting the populace against its own safeguards. Instead John Howard and Kim Beazley couldn't get down that path fast enough. The end point of such a strategy is unknowable, especially when the context may be a global war footing.

Both major parties have now deserted the position that is most necessary in representative governments – being able to have a longer perspective and a cooler head than the blindly reactive sections of the general public, working off the skewed and inadequate information of the tabloids and talkback. Consequently, the most pressing political need is for a new alliance of people who recognise the dangers of this and are willing to make issues of liberty and independence a prime political concern.

There is a need for a greater formalisation of the links and alliances that have formed across existing Left and Right camps for the preservation of civil liberties and of a public sphere where the full range of political opinion and action is conceivable. I am not suggesting a new political party – the last thing we need is another political party – but I am suggesting that the project of preserving our most basic political and civil freedoms is the most pressing one for citizens who care about genuine responsibility in government. Differences of opinion about economic and cultural questions must take a back seat in the concerted effort to preserve and extend the fundamental political freedom we must assert at the moment even to debate these other matters.

Political liberty has always been fragile in Australia, because it has been so automatically assumed. Our constitution is a document that is over-whelmingly oriented to questions of trade (to the freedom of things) rather than politics – the freedom of persons. The suppression of opin-ion is largely unknown in the roll call of Australian history, because the debates around the iniquities perpetrated were so ad hoc, and based on no transcendent revolutionary narrative, as with the Americans.

Neither major political party has consistently presented itself as the champion of political freedom in Australia. Under Evatt, the ALP defeated the Communist Party Dissolution Bill, with its promise of savage political repression, yet it was a Liberal, Don Chipp, who broke the hold of censorship in Australia. For a generation – from the ascension of Whitlam to the end of the Keating era – the ALP presented itself as a party concerned with the extension of freedom (in the form of such things as equal opportunity as well as political structures), but it has now retreated to a position that is pre-'60s, and even pre-Evatt. So now there is no major impediment to whatever tidal wave of further reaction may roll in from the American earthquake. Those who think that proposition alarmist are invited to imagine how they would tell the person they were three months ago of all that happened during two weeks in September, where it left us, and where we are likely to end up. The times are too dangerous, the air is too filled with the gasoline smell of reaction for there to be too much prevarication about old feuds or past histories, for diffidence about élitism, or reservations about the chattering classes or any of that nonsense. We are all aligned against the forces of reaction – and they now stretch from media magnates and redneck populists to Kim Beazley and John Faulkner – and fighting for the most basic conditions of a pluralist political society. Whether or not he leaves the Lodge on November 10, that is John Howard's legacy to Australia – that he secured and cemented, he deepened and entrenched, so much of the worst, rather than the best, of the country he so haphazardly came to lead.

SOURCES

Essay sources and occasional supplementary material are given below. Page numbers indicate where the arguments appear.

2   The best account of Arne Rinnen's decision appeared in the *Age*, 2 September 2001.

2   Bill Farmer's testimony can be found at www.fedcourt.gov.au, Vadarlis v. Commonwealth of Australia.

3   John Howard's press gallery quote was reprinted in the *Australian*, 4 September 2001.

5   Howard as 'Iron John' appeared on the cover of the *Bulletin*, 11 September 2001.

5   Beazley's later decision to pass an amended version of the Border Protection Bill effectively blocked any appeal to the High Court, despite the fact that two Federal Court justices had found for the refugees and two had found against.

6   Editorial quote from the *Wall Street Journal* was reprinted in the *Australian Financial Review*, 3 September 2001.

7   For a full transcript of Ruddock's comments, see 'Ruddock Replies to Community Concerns', interview with Philip Ruddock and Kerry O'Brien, *7.30 Report*, ABC Television, 14 August 2001, http://www.abc.net.au/7.30/s346319.htm.

7   The most recent example of this form of US neo-conservatism can be seen in David Horowitz's article following the World Trade Center bombings, implicitly blaming the culture of '60s radicalism for lack of American consensus regarding response to the attack. See 'Bin Laden's American Blood Brothers', 17 September 2001, http://www.salon.com.

8   John Howard quote broadcast on PM, ABC Radio, 1 August 1988.

8   John Stone quoted in the *Herald* (Melbourne), 9 August 1988.

9   For a demythologising view of the Fraser years, see Charles Richardson's 'The Fraser Years' in J.R. Nethercote's *Liberalism and the Australian Federation*, Federation Press, 2001.

10   It should be noted that Ruddock also crossed the floor to vote with Labor on equal opportunities. He has crossed a fair way back since then.

11   Howard described himself as 'liberal' on *Meet the Press*, Network Ten, 6 March 1994, as 'radical' in the *Age*, 4 May 1992, and as a 'Burkean conservative' in the *Age*, 8 July 1994.

14   Howard quotes in order of appearance: transcript of Howard–Peacock press conference, 17 July 1987; 'Foreword' in Nethercote, p.v; Alfred Deakin lecture, 1986, p.3; *The Age*, 8 July 1994; address to the Committee for Melbourne, 18 July 1995 (unpublished typescript).

15   Howard quotes from Nethercote, p.vi–vii.

15   For a more extensive account of this aspect of the Reagan years, see Peggy Noonan's *What I Saw at the Revolution*, Random House, New York, 1990. Noonan was a speechwriter for Ronald Reagan.

17   For more on the theme of unity, see G. Hage's 'Ayatollah Johnny's Australian Fundamentalism' *Arena Magazine*, No. 51, pp.27–32.

19   Howard quoted in the *Australian*, 29 June 1994.

20–21   The draft preamble to the Constitution (1999) is reprinted in Donald Horne's *Looking for Leadership*, Viking, 2001.

22   It should be noted that some Aboriginal groups would insist on being considered as 'outside the nation' too. The difference here is that there is an attempt to define them as both in and outside the nation.

23   For a full discussion of the concept of 'positive freedom' see Isaiah Berlin's *Four Essays on Liberty*, Oxford University Press, 1969.

25   Howard's full quote – 'I'm glad people are at least able to say these things without being accused of racism and bigotry.' – appears in Robert Manne's *The Barren Years*, Text, 2001, p.38.

26   Pauline Hanson's speech to the House of Representatives, 10 September 1996, is quoted in Horne, pp.277–278.

26–27   Howard quotes in order of appearance: Speech to the Liberal State Council of NSW, 28 October 1995; Speech to St Paul's School Queensland, 10 July 1998, quoted in Hage; Sir John Monash lecture, 1993, p.3.

27   Robert Menzies 'The Forgotten People' wartime radio talk, quoted in Horne, p.102.

29   This is not merely a right-wing thing. The centre-left slant of some ABC radio shows is also a form of 'self-constitution' albeit a minority one. Furthermore the commercial stations manage their callers in a far more cynical and deliberate fashion.

29   For more on the relationship between 'nation building' and the media see Paul James's *Nation Formation*, Sage, London, 1996.

30   Whitlam's reluctance is detailed in his book *The Truth of the Matter*, Penguin, 1979.

30   More on Howard and the immigration debate can be found in Humphrey McQueen's column in the *Bulletin*, 21 September 2001.

31   See Anne Davies and Helen Trinca, *Waterfront: The Battle that Changed Australia*, Doubleday, 2000, for more information on the docklands dispute.

31   For more on 'economic treason', see the *Australian*, 3 August 2001, 'Car Strike Treason to Spread'.

33   Howard quote from his speech to Business Community Breakfast, Perth, 11 July 1995.

33   Statistics provided in ABS, Balance of Payments and International Investment Position, Australia (5302.0).

33   John Edwards from his *Australia's Economic Revolution*, UNSW Press, p.10.

34   Details of tariff wall reductions can be found in Paul Kelly's 'Labour and Globalisation' from Robert Manne's *The Australian Century: Political Struggle in the Building of a Nation*, published by Text, 1999.

35–36   For an overview, see Botsman and Latham, *The Enabling State*, Pluto, 2000.

38   For more on the 'Australian settlement', see Paul Kelly's *The End of Certainty*, Allen & Unwin, 1992.

38   Michelle Gunn, 'Back to the Future is Passé' in Paul Kelly (ed.) *Future Tense*, Allen & Unwin, 1999, pp.139–152. Apps quoted in Gunn, p.147.

38–39   'Towards an Economic Policy for the Family' address to the Council for the National Interest, 7 March 1994.

40   Fukuyama, F., *Trust*, Free Press, 1995.

44   The intellectual framework for this section – and for much of this essay – is derived from the work done by many of the writers in the 'Arena' group, published in *Arena Magazine* and *Arena Journal*.

44–45   Peter Costello, 'The Spirit of the Volunteer', Sir Henry Bolte Lecture, 15 August 2001.

45   It should be noted that there are many dissenters from the fundamentally critical position here associated with Putnam and Sennett (and also with neo-conservative critics such as Neil Postman and Francis Fukuyama). Most of these come from a 'postmodern' perspective, arguing that such critiques mistake hitherto existing forms of socialisation for the only possible forms, thereby failing to acknowledge new and effective modes of social life – ones that involve self-development, negotiation and fluidity.

51   Latham, M., *What Did You Learn Today*, Allen & Unwin, 2001, p.64.

52   Akerman on *Insiders*, ABC TV, Sunday 30 September 2001.

54   *Business Review Weekly*, 'CEOs Back Howard' 6–12 September 2001, p.74.

55   Keating on *Lateline*, ABC TV, Tuesday 2 September 2001.

from Mark Aarons

John Birmingham has been roundly criticised by several reviewers for not being in possession of all the facts that formed Australian policy on East Timor from 1974 to 1999. Essentially, such critics argue that behind-the-scenes debates were much more complex and subtle than Birmingham's account. In his essay, Birmingham mainly relies on the Howard government's recent release of official documents from the 1970s (dealing with the period of the Whitlam government), and on the far more limited official material available on the 1998–99 period (most of it leaked by the intelligence community).

In relation to the mid-1970s period, the broad outline of the policy debate has, in fact, been known for over twenty years. In 1980, Richard Walsh and the late George Munster published their extraordinary book of leaked Foreign Affairs and Defence documents (*Documents on Australian Defence and Foreign Policy, 1968–1975*). The book included a highly revealing selection of documents dealing with Australian policy towards Indonesia and East Timor during the government of Gough Whitlam. Indeed, the revelations contained in this book were so embarrassing that Whitlam's successor, Malcolm Fraser, had it suppressed by taking legal action in the courts. I would argue that there was more involved in this censorship than the usual official obsession with hiding unpleasant secrets for as long as possible (although this was a major element in the court case).

Contrary to popular portrayals of Australian policy, I have long believed that unlocking the secret history of Australia's complicity in the East Timor tragedy should more properly focus on Fraser's government, not on Whitlam's. The latter was a Labor Prime Minister and this probably explains the obsession that many Australians have had with his role in the Timor tragedy. The East Timor support movement was, of course, based mainly on the left of politics (although not exclusively, as Michael Hodgman and John Dowd demonstrate). This has resulted in too much attention being focused on Whitlam, and far too little on his successor. After all, the most trenchant critics often come from within the family, although it has suited the conservative side of politics to point to Whitlam's East Timor policies to justify their own amoral and predictably unsuccessful policies.

Indeed, I would argue that Malcolm Fraser's determination to protect Whitlam's secrets by suppressing the Walsh/Munster book in 1980 actually reveals more about his desire to cover up his own vastly greater culpability in the East Timor events than anything else. This is a point entirely missed in Birmingham's otherwise broadly accurate portrayal of official Australian policy. That he missed this critical element probably arises more from the absence of official records than lack of diligence, but there is still plenty of evidence for those who want to review the public record. The problem also arises because of Fraser's continuing silence on the subject, in contrast to Whitlam's increasingly bombastic and ever more unconvincing defence of his own shabby role. In light of Fraser's overall positive record of supporting anti-racist and humanitarian causes, his Timor policy remains (like Whitlam's) an enigma, which (if uncorrected) will inevitably result in history judging him harshly.

Whitlam's role has, of course, been widely analysed and properly criticised. Indeed, Fraser's suppression of the Walsh/Munster documents did not come soon enough to prevent the truth about Whitlam and his key bureaucratic advisor (Richard Woolcott, Australian Ambassador to Jakarta) coming out. Enough copies of the book had already found their way into the public arena before the court ordered its withdrawal. Although the suppression of the book included an effective gag on media reporting, the Walsh/Munster documents have been widely discussed (including in my own 1992 book co-authored with Robert Domm: *East Timor: A Western Made Tragedy*). In fact, the Walsh/Munster collection includes many of those on which Birmingham relies so heavily, especially the infamous Woolcott cable of August 1975 and the much more accurate predictions of the Defence Department's Bill Pritchett of the following October. Although the selection of 1970s documents released by the Howard government in the aftermath of the 1999 independence referendum adds to our knowledge, the essentials have been well known and much analysed over the last twenty years. In this sense, Birmingham's polemic merely refines an already well established and powerful critique of Australian foreign policy that long ago laid bare the foolishness and futility of Woolcott's advice, and Whitlam's intellectual and policy bankruptcy in following it.

Where I much more seriously depart from Birmingham's account is that it seems to me he has fallen into the trap identified by Labor's current shadow Foreign Minister, Laurie Brereton. In criticising the Howard government's highly selective release of the Timor files in 2000, Brereton rightly highlighted

Howard's deliberate policy to protect the reputation of Malcolm Fraser by refusing to open the records of his administration. By choosing to restrict his analysis to the 1974–75 and 1998–99 periods, Birmingham effectively misses Fraser's complicity in the genocide of East Timor between 1975 and 1978 (when the population was reduced by approximately one-third, and the policies of cultural extermination were devised and first implemented).

Although Birmingham makes some broad references to the policies pursued by Fraser (and for that matter, his Labor successors), the detail actually matters. For a start, it should never be forgotten that Malcolm Fraser was Prime Minister at the time of the Indonesian invasion (7 December 1975). True, he was only in caretaker mode, but was elected with a massive majority six days later. Once in office as the legitimate Prime Minister, Fraser not only followed Whitlam's lead but also introduced key elements to Australia's Timor policy that were far nastier than Labor's. For example, it was Fraser who effectively cut off the resistance from the outside world. Prior to the invasion, Fretilin had put in place a rudimentary network, both for internal and external communications. Using simple Single Side Band radios, the resistance planned to keep in touch both with its units operating throughout the rugged interior of the country and with the rest of the world. The effectiveness of this decision is illustrated by the radio reports made by Fretilin's Alarico Fernandes even as the invasion was in its first hours. Fernandes's accounts of Indonesian atrocities on 7 December were broadcast by the Australian media, thus threatening to keep the world's attention on the war that was then raging in and around Dili.

History records that the Fraser government and its senior bureaucrats fell over themselves to stop the two-way communications. At first, Telecom received Fernandes's transmissions as legitimate communications, logging them and passing them to the nominated recipients (as had been the case for some weeks prior to the invasion). Soon after the election on 13 December 1975, the government stepped in and ordered Telecom to cut the link. Just as the first wave of mass killings started, the only alternative version to Indonesia's claim of 'peaceful incorporation' was officially silenced. This was no accident, nor was it done in ignorance of the facts. Indeed, Australia's signals intelligence agency, the Defence Signals Directorate (DSD) was closely monitoring both the Fretilin and Indonesian Army radio traffic. The resulting intelligence landed on the desks of both the Prime Minister and the Minister for Defence. This confirmed the basic accuracy of Fretilin's claims of the campaign of mass killings, rape, torture and brutality aimed at the civilian population that was engulfing East Timor in December 1975 and January 1976.

The determination of the Fraser government to follow Woolcott's August 1975 advice to 'minimise the public impact' of Indonesia's aggression (to quote his cable) is illustrated by what happened next. When supporters of Timorese independence – led by Denis Freney and other communists, myself included – bought new transmitters and re-established contact with the resistance, the Fraser government threw a vast array of forces into the battle to re-silence the voice beaming the truth out of the country. DSD, ASIO, the Commonwealth and State (Special Branch) police forces and the Department of Communications were all detailed to collect intelligence on our activities and break up the network we had established in order to cut off the information flow. Telephones were tapped around the country, radio experts and sophisticated electronic equipment were dispatched to the Northern Territory to track down the radios and their operators, and close physical surveillance was employed in the government operation to silence the resistance. Code breakers were brought in, both to break the rudimentary codes we had established to communicate among ourselves and (more importantly) those used by Fretilin for passing secret information from the interior to their leaders who had been sent out of the country prior to the invasion.

These official operations were not simply the usual manifestation of Cold War anti-communism, and even less were they straightforward domestic law enforcement. They were directed from the very top of both the government and the foreign affairs and intelligence bureaucracies precisely to assist the Indonesian government to achieve its goal of destroying the East Timorese resistance, free from the prying eyes of the outside world. In this they were successful. Despite several arrests of those involved in the underground radio operation, it was kept going for several years after the invasion (and even revived intermittently during the 1980s). However, the legitimacy of the information passed through this clandestine channel was invariably questioned, both by the media and the wider international community. Jakarta's genocidal policies went largely unreported for the crucial three years during which the worst mass killings occurred. The news that was reported was almost always qualified, thus diminishing the veracity of the claims.

The Fraser government's insistence on silencing the voice of the resistance was matched by its diplomatic role. While ostensibly joining with the rest of the world in deploring the use of force and calling for a peaceful resolution, Australia actively aided Jakarta in many ways, most notably to isolate the victims. An early indication of the Fraser government's determination to assist Suharto involved undermining the UN's pathetic efforts to intervene. In late December 1975, the UN dispatched Italian diplomat Winspeare Gucciardi on a fact-finding mission to East Timor. The diplomat was given a 'guided tour' by the Indonesian military, which predictably prevented Gucciardi from crossing the frontline to visit the resistance. Gucciardi responded to Jakarta's determination to frustrate his mission by approaching the Fraser government and requesting assistance. Fretilin had illustrated the importance of its radio link by broadcasting an invitation for Gucciardi to visit them by flying into the country to specially prepared airfields, the precise locations of which would be held back until the mission was about to take off, or even until it was in the air.

The UN diplomat apparently thought this central to his mission and asked Canberra to provide a plane to allow him to complete his task. The Fraser government flatly turned him down, citing 'safety' concerns. Gucciardi was forced to abandon his mission without consulting the other major party to the conflict. The Fraser government had not only failed to strongly support the UN mission, but had effectively isolated the resistance from the international community and silenced the legitimate voice of East Timor. The troublesome radio link had almost put Fretilin in the middle of a diplomatic peace initiative under UN auspices. An on-the-ground visit would have exposed Jakarta's lies about the warm welcome its army had received, and the lack of opposition to integration except from a few 'communist' malcontents in the hills. (In fact, two-thirds of the population – about 400,000 people from mainly peasant families – had put themselves under the protection of Fretilin, a fact that both the Fraser and Suharto governments wanted suppressed.)

Fraser's co-operation with Suharto on these (and many other) matters was vital in the following three years. It enabled the Indonesian Army to undertake its murderous work without the nuisance of the international opprobrium that followed the 1991 Santa Cruz cemetery massacre and the killings and destruction both before and after the 1999 act of self-determination. In light of the scale of the killings and civilian suffering between December 1975 and December 1978 (when the resistance briefly collapsed) both Santa Cruz and the 1999 events must be viewed as minor incidents in the era of Indonesian occupation.

The complicity and guilt of the Fraser government and its senior bureaucrats, I would argue, is thereby far greater than either Whitlam's or Fraser's Labor (and Liberal) successors. The government's intelligence services listened in while an act of genocide on the scale of the Nazis' 'Final Solution' occurred right on Australia's doorstep. It should be recalled that one in three Jews died under Hitler, while at least one in three East Timorese died under Suharto, perhaps more. These deaths resulted not only from mass killings, but from a famine deliberately induced by the Indonesians and as a result of counter-insurgency operations that were supported both by Western equipment (particularly purpose-designed planes and helicopters) and specialist anti-guerrilla training (provided mainly by the United States at that time, later by Australia, too). The campaign of killings was accompanied by a deliberate policy of cultural genocide, involving forcible population relocations (into what were, essentially, concentration camps), repression of traditional languages and culture and the 'Indonesianisation' of the territory, especially the economy and education. Like the Churchill, Stalin and Roosevelt governments before it, the Fraser government actively hid the truth both from Australians and the rest of the world and prevented any action that could have at least ameliorated the suffering.

There is no doubt the truth was known to the government. Former intelligence officers have confided to me that throughout these crucial three years the radio traffic of both sides of the war (the Indonesian Army and Fretilin) was recorded, transcribed, decoded (where necessary) and passed up the chain of command until it landed on the responsible ministers' desks. Little wonder, then, that Alexander Downer was reluctant to release the secret files of the Fraser years. Until all the files (including the top-secret signals intelligence reports) are available for public scrutiny and analysis, the full extent of Australia's appeasement of Indonesia and complicity in the East Timor tragedy will, in fact, not be known. What is known is that Fraser waited until the resistance briefly collapsed in late 1978 and then hastily extended *de jure* recognition to Jakarta's forcible incorporation of East Timor into Indonesia, something that our closest Western allies refused to do. Australia's diplomats then engaged in a campaign to assist Suharto to have the East Timor issue removed from the international agenda, especially at the UN. This campaign almost succeeded, with the active assistance of Fraser's predecessor, Gough Whitlam, who travelled to the UN to argue the case for Indonesia.

There is a compelling case that the Fraser years (especially the period from December 1975 to December 1978) are the most crucial in uncovering the deeper motivations that subsequently led a string of governments (of both sides) to continue the discredited Whitlam/Fraser policies that have shamed Australia internationally (and worse, to ourselves). That John Birmingham missed this critical point reduces his otherwise well-intentioned and well-written polemic to the bookends of the story.

Mark Aarons

from Frank Brennan

Working in East Timor this last year, I was looking forward to settling into *Appeasing Jakarta*, the second *Quarterly Essay*, during a one-week visit across the border to the refugee camps in West Timor. Given past involvement in Aboriginal issues, my expectation was heightened by a fulsome correspondence between your first essayist and his interlocutors focused on *In Denial*. Naturally I was impressed by the writing of Birmingham, Manne and some of his inter-locutors. But I am left with an eerie dissatisfaction – I am pleased to be away from it all, and yet, here I am in midst of it! In John Birmingham's essay we hear nothing from the Timorese themselves and in the Manne correspondence we hear little from Aborigines. Their voices and experiences as insiders would have blunted the moral message for and about complicit outsiders. The tone of the writing is the righteousness which is reserved for outside commentators writing with the benefit of hindsight, assuming that the political actors at the time had a clear choice between good and evil.

One major difference between Australia's conduct in 1975 and 1999 in rela-tion to East Timor and Indonesia was that this time Australian officials, including Ambassador John McCarthy, did consult and dialogue with key Timorese actors who themselves made assessments about the risks of sustained, systematic violence from the TNI and their militia allies, and who themselves urged the continuation of the popular consultation process subject to the flawed condi-tions set down in the May 5 agreement to which Australia was not a party and to which Portugal as a party had presumably given agreement only after approval by the key Timorese actors. No matter how appeasing our attitude to Jakarta, our government's position was in line with that espoused by the Timorese leader-ship. I do not hear Timorese people in East Timor complaining about Australia appeasing Jakarta during 1999. Though they might not have access to all the Canberra information available to John Birmingham and William Maley, they do have a lifetime of experience of Jakarta's way of doing business. Even with hindsight and after all the suffering, the major sentiment of the Timorese towards us Australians regarding the events of 1999 is one of gratitude. At least this time, the erstwhile appeaser listened to the victim and acted in a manner judged appropriate by the victim and not altogether in the appeaser's self interest. In moral terms this must count for something. I do not deny that there was a failure to share all intelligence and that things could have been done better. Even if all intelligence had been shared (and I am one prepared to assume there are good as well as bad reasons for withholding it), I think the Timorese leaders would still have urged that the popular consultation proceed even if the terms of the May 5 agreement remained unamendable and fraught with difficulty.

Birmingham says, 'The question of war crimes is looming as a new touchstone for Australian realism.' The UN has already told the Timorese that an international war crimes tribunal is not a goer. The Security Council is just not interested and sadly there is not a proven, credible court system on either side of the border. The only hope of bringing those in Indonesia to justice is the local prosecution of the 23 named in the Indonesian human rights report. There are three levels of offenders: senior TNI officers, key militia leaders, and the small fry militia. Only the third level is within reach of authorities outside Indonesia. Some key militia leaders will return and come into the net when the UN leaves town and when the East Timor government and militia leaders cut a deal. It will be the sort of deal which will not withstand much scrutiny from your essayists. But it may bring home the remaining refugees, including the little people who are the pawns beyond the reach of the international community since the killing of the UNHCR workers in September 2000. Once again, Timorese actors will be active participants in the moral calculus about intentions and outcomes.

On the Aboriginal front, it is common ground between Robert Manne and all his white intellectual interlocutors that any 'genocidal dimension in child removal came to an end' in the post-war period. Presumably public debate about the correct classification of the pre-war policy will continue, each side being equally convinced and passionate about its position. But none of this conviction and passion will change the lives of present-day Aboriginal Australians, nor will it contribute to a resolution of the outstanding issues. The Bringing them home report highlighted that there is still a disproportionate number of Aboriginal children in need of State intervention for their care and protection. The principle of placement with Aboriginal families is readily accepted. But this simply means disproportionate burdens being placed on functional Aboriginal families. Speak to anyone involved in Aboriginal welfare and health and you will hear how unaddressed are the present-day problems. The writings of Aboriginal leaders Pat Dodson and Marcia Langton in the Royal Commission into Aboriginal Deaths in Custody put beyond doubt the cycle of violence in so many Aboriginal families and communities.

Being a Jesuit, I have no fear of public debate about morality but I do side with Inga Clendinnen in apprehending that the moralism of our public intellectuals about our pre-war past may be discouraging the subtlety of analysis and 'patience and generosity in judgment' required not only to get our history right (which is her primary concern) but also if we as a nation are to rectify the present abuses of Aboriginal children (this being my primary concern).

Whatever of the political campaign against Bringing them home, those of us supportive of greater justice for Aborigines need to concede the following points. To date, all test cases in the courts on the stolen generations have been abysmal failures despite the provision of all necessary public funds for the conduct of the litigation. There is no political basis for the establishment of a reparations tribunal until there has been at least one successful case in the courts. With reparations, we are back where we were with land rights in 1971. At that time, Aborigines lost their test case in the courts. The newly elected Whitlam government decided to take the matter from the courts and into its own hands after the conduct of a royal commission. (A new Labor government could do the same for the stolen generations.) But even then, there was no real commitment to national land rights until the successful win in Mabo in 1992. Mabo created the political imperative for action by the Keating government because industry groups wanted certainty. A successful stolen generations case may create the imperative for a reparations tribunal. Meanwhile the real moral ambiguities will be addressed by those Aborigines and their fellow Australians wanting to improve the conditions of Aboriginal families and communities. The ongoing debate in various white intellectual circles (from the Bennelong Society to the Quarterly Essay circle) about the correct classification of pre-war practices will continue but let it not provide an excuse for those who are not Aboriginal simply doing nothing as outsiders, in the name of self-determination.

The moralism of these essays will be justified if we writers and readers are further compelled to do something to put right the ongoing effects of past appeasement and assimilation. Chances are that whatever we do will be morally fraught and ambiguous. That is why the issues are so hard, deserving a Quarterly Essay or two after we have all given it our best shot. Meanwhile, I look forward to an essay written by an insider.

Frank Brennan

from Duncan Campbell

John Birmingham's essay, *Appeasing Jakarta*, with its powerful emotional backing, is an unusual contribution to understanding a sustained foreign policy failure. I share his central view that, 'for as long as Indonesia remains an unstable and potentially authoritarian state, elemental political differences will inevitably preclude a close and abiding relationship,' although it is hardly the 'heresy' Birmingham claims. You cannot build a stable relationship with an unstable partner. But unfortunately, like the poisoned wells in East Timor on which it draws, the essay's appeal is adulterated.

Of course those who choose to live in the public limelight also risk exposure in the public stocks. Birmingham nevertheless debases his case on Australia's handling of Timor by aiming so much argument *ad hominem* at Richard Woolcott and, to a surprisingly lesser extent, at Gough Whitlam. Not only that, but the substantive criticism of policy making around the 1975 crisis is skewed off course. Nor is it worth becoming maudlin about our moral failures over self-determination in Timor. Aboriginal Australians have been utterly failed on this score, and our record in PNG was not all we claimed.

Whitlam or Woolcott are no longer the issue, but by insisting that they are, and denying that he is doing so, Birmingham contributes more confusion, asks some wrong questions, and will leave many Australians as emotionally and intellectually distracted and divergently inclined over Timor as ever. Indonesia, not Timor, was and remains the central issue for Australia. The challenge, which Birmingham fails to meet, is to express the relevance of the two in terms to provide continuity of policy guidance.

Birmingham's central assertion that Woolcott was wrong and culpable in assuming that an Indonesian takeover would provide a viable (even if vicious) outcome reflects an unsound analysis of policy history that shows little understanding of the world as it was in the 1970s, or of the then parameters of possibility for Australia. The contrary assumption would have been less valid because no alternative control over the territory was forthcoming, and certainly none acceptable to Indonesia, ASEAN or Australia at the end of 1975.

Earlier in 1975 I had represented the UN committee on decolonisation at the independence ceremonies for another Portuguese island territory, Sao Tome and Principe, and had flown down the West African coast from Lisbon with a 'Red Admiral' who, it was widely feared, would soon head a communist Portugal. His chances were spiked over that very weekend but Portugal's future was a near-run thing at a crucial stage of the Cold War. The continuing fratricide that the Portuguese bequeathed to Timor as they left, the chance of a Communist grab for power in Dili, and regional responses to the crisis can only be understood, as they all occurred, in the dominant context of the Cold War. The motivating ideology was anti-Communism, not nationalism or anti-colonialism – despite the strength of the last. Birmingham assists the debate by referring to West Irian, but not by glossing over the consideration that the USA, having contrived to give that territory to Sukarno out of fear that otherwise he would pass Indonesia to Communist control, was not about to alienate the anti-Communist Suharto over Timor.

This was indeed a time of accelerated decolonisation under UN pressure. Its grab of Timor cost Indonesia the leadership in New York, which it was about to inherit from Tanzania, of UN activity in this key political area, and lost it considerable influence in the non-aligned world. But Suharto, Murdani, et al., were playing another game, with exclusively anti-Communist cards.

The year was also the one when we rushed to terminate the trusteeship agreement covering PNG. Seemingly there was a great divergence in Australian foreign policy during the last quarter of 1975, when we claimed to be as conscientious in thrusting self-determination on the peoples of PNG as we were callous in denying it to the East Timorese. This is an appearance which, given all the moralizing about Timor, needs to be questioned.

The Timor debate has centred on Woolcott's juxtaposition of pragmatism with principle, in this case self-determination. But wouldn't an examination of our approach to PNG that year suggest the same position? Independence was rushed at the last (Labor) minute in PNG, less because the territory was ready to make an informed and timely move to self-management than because we couldn't wait to be seen to have discharged our colonial responsibilities or to escape the possibility of presiding over bloodshed there. We handed over in Port Moresby for pragmatic, politically correct reasons. We basked in New York as practising decolonisers. But as for faithful discharge of principle, even the UN representatives of the Soviet bloc satellites surmised that we were pulling out too soon.

The truth is we needed significantly more acceptance of international principle in both Timor and PNG precisely because that is where our longer term policy interests lay. We failed to bind ourselves, let alone the Indonesians, to eventual self-determination for the East Timorese, and to proceed on the basis that the future in Timor had to be relatively trouble free, something that could only be ensured with the consent of the governed. The central policy consideration ought to have been that Timor constituted too great a threat to maintaining, let alone developing, our relations with Indonesia to be left unattended. It was too dangerous to duck. The importance of Indonesia to Australia demanded that the issues in Timor be confronted, not conceded. By taking the immediate soft option we risked, and ultimately almost wrecked, the overall relationship. The failure of professional policy advising lay in the acceptance of that risk over Timor without re-insurance. Birmingham says that Woolcott was right to oppose a policy on Indonesia and Timor constructed in moral terms. But that was never the issue. The issue was the practical one that, without self-determination, Timor could forever impair much more important dealings with Jakarta. We should have been on the UN bandwagon from the beginning, pushing Indonesia to report on its administration of Timor, advocating regular UN visiting missions, preparing for a secure act of self-determination that would stick, and committing the Security Council to responsibility for it, right from the beginning. The UN would have afforded us some insulation from the heat generated by friction over Timor. The more we ducked self-determination, the more we placed at risk the very management of the vital relationship with Jakarta. And that is surely the central lesson of Timor from both 1975 and 1999. The line of principle was the only practical choice for a policy with any future.

Not all your readers will recognize that Bill Pritchett and Gordon Jockel, whom Birmingham quotes with approval in this case (as would I), were both Foreign Affairs (or pedantically External Affairs) born and bred. They are two of a number who illustrate the tunnel vision of a bureaucratic Canberra view, which has obviously misled Birmingham, that monolithic and errant advice from Foreign Affairs prevailed tragically in the Whitlam and Howard governments and in the time between them. Much contemporary comment that he quotes towards the end of the essay is petty and partisan. For a policy-oriented contribution it is also pointless. More's the pity because Birmingham is so right in nailing an 'aspirational' approach to Indonesia policy. In no other foreign policy field have we suffered so grievously from this affliction. For almost thirty years of the relationship with the Republic of Indonesia we have fallen for the siren song of over-achievement there, that we can do better and bigger things than should ever have been believed or attempted. I share the contrary view that our Indonesia policy advising would be safer in the hands of specialists in worst-case scenarios. Paul Keating's 'historic' security treaty with Suharto is the worst example of engorged policy towards Indonesia and Birmingham rightly nails it. Treated seriously, it had feet of clay. Treated suspiciously, the sniggers from the inner circle of Foreign Affairs and Defence negotiators in the loop that it would win the coming election against John Howard made it disgraceful diplomacy dishonestly presented.

The folly of promoting a pro-Defence view against the Foreign Affairs and Trade record lies largely in the overall record of the Defence group itself, which embraced its relationship with the Indonesian armed forces with a truly myopic zeal. So open were we to co-operating that the Indonesians were able to convert our human intelligence channels and the policy counsel of our too numerous colonels into an unfiltered conveyor belt on which what was loaded as Jakarta propaganda at one end came off as policy proposals to Canberra at the other. And at times the diplomatic and defence lines were indistinguishable. One of our ambassadors, also responsible for pulling the plug in PNG, promoted himself to Indonesia on the strength of knowing Murdani.

Because of inherent instability at the Indonesian end, and if you would believe Birmingham, chronic inability on the Australian side, and in fact in any event, the central task of Indonesia policy is the very management of this vital relationship. Not in the predictable future will it be to seek great new outcomes, save to maximize mutual respect. The secret of management will be to concentrate on identifying, and facing up to, the major obstacles of destructive capacity that arise along the way.

The Timor problem had finally to be surmounted in 1999 for the reason that it had reached the point of menacing the whole relationship with Indonesia. Had we been prepared to be agent for the Security Council before the referendum, the wounds to be healed with Indonesia, not to mention those in Timor, would have been smaller.

Over the next several years Indonesia may well need international help and intervention, some of it unwelcome, in order to remain intact. Aceh apart, the problems will be mainly in the east. This will be the period for Australia to make a contribution to Indonesia, and to our inescapable mutual relationship, marked by principle, internationalism, and domestic commitment, essentially in the spirit of our initial support for Indonesian independence. We need a fresh start, but the political leadership required is not in view.

Duncan Campbell

from Tony Kevin

Birmingham's essay offers an illogical and unsustainable analysis of Australia's role in East Timor's tragic transition to independence in 1999, in arguing (pp. 57–64) that Australia's (to be specific, DFAT's) mindset of appeasing Indonesia was a major cause of the East Timorese people's sufferings in this period.

The appeasement critique cannot plausibly be applied to the new policy environment opened up by the ALP's 1998 decision to reject Australia's prior bipartisan *de jure* recognition of East Timor's incorporation, and to call for a genuine act of self-determination under international supervision. The Howard government took the domestic political decision to follow suit, and to try to begin such a process. Initially, Howard wanted 5 or 10 years of preparation for an act of self-determination (so did Xanana Gusmao and Bishop Belo).

But Howard in January 1999 decided (without consulting any East Timorese) to go along with Habibie's direction to expedite the whole process to reach a conclusion in 1999 during his interim presidency. Wiranto's anti-independence group in TNI and their client militias also supported Habibie's position, because they expected that over the next few months they could successfully bribe or intimidate enough East Timorese into voting against independence in the UN-supervised referendum, so as finally to give international legitimacy to Indonesia's annexation of East Timor in 1975.

Downer and Howard had a pretty shrewd idea from Australian aid and religious people in East Timor, and from other intelligence, that the vote was likely to go for independence. The policy challenge for Australia was to keep Indonesia on board the process, at least until it was set firm by the 5 May UN–Portugal–Indonesia agreement to set up UNAMET. Hence Downer's refusal to acknowledge the reality of TNI's support of militia atrocities from February until well into April; the 'rogue elements' defence, and so on.

This was not a matter of appeasement, but of deliberately turning a blind eye to obvious ongoing atrocities, in the interests of the bigger objective of keeping the UN vote timetable moving forward.

Although UN Secretary-General Kofi Annan had repeatedly emphasised to the UN Security Council in the earlier part of 1999 that a safe security environment was 'a prerequisite' before he would certify that the election could go ahead, Australia put Annan under great pressure after the May agreement to set these considerations aside – arguing that this window of opportunity for a genuine act of self-determination might not come again, and that considerations of 'logistics' (i.e. violence and intimidation against East Timorese people in the lead-up to the vote) should not be allowed to delay the timetable.

In response (Australia was the expert on East Timor, after all), Annan quietly dropped the security prerequisite from his regular progress reports to the Security Council. The security issue was increasingly fudged by the UN. In July, Annan assured the Council that the people's security situation would improve because Indonesian government authorities were promising it would. (It never did.) Then in August, Annan and Downer rationalised the whole problem away: while they acknowledged that there had been major intimidation and violence during the months leading up to the vote, they were now satisfied that election procedures had been sufficiently set in place for a valid democratic act of self-determination on 30 August.

On the eve of the vote, Annan promised the East Timorese people that UNAMET would not desert them (though on 8 September, it very nearly did). Immediately after the result had been declared on 4 September, before the main retaliatory violence had begun, Downer congratulated himself that, 'Australia had calibrated this pretty well all along' and an anonymous senior Australian diplomat in Dili commented, 'We just might wing this.'

The issue during these months of 1999 is in no way about appeasement of Indonesia. Rather, it is about Australia's disingenuous manipulation, in the style of a puppet-master, of Indonesian and UN behaviour in order to move matters towards a particular objective: the opportunity for the East Timorese effectively to exercise a real vote on self-determination, notwithstanding Indonesia's insistence on maintaining control of security during the process (a trust that Indonesian local officials were manifestly abusing).

The really important questions about what Australia was doing in those eight months are obscured by Birmingham's tired anti-DFAT appeasement polemic. This was a quite new game, and Australia played it very differently from in the past; that's perhaps why the Wiranto group failed to see through it until it was too late. Wiranto thought he was bluffing the Australians: in reality, they were double-bluffing him. By appearing publicly to shrug off dreadful acts of TNI-supported militia violence in the early months especially (Alas, Suai, Liquica,

Dili), Downer and DFAT were nursing Indonesia along into being locked into the timetable for the UN-supervised vote on 30 August: that was the 'big picture' Australian strategy, and in the end it worked.

Downer hoped that, at the end of the day, Wiranto as a rationalist political actor would see the game was up and (perhaps after the militia had vented their spleen with a little cathartic post-vote violence: 'there were always going to be some casualties') would throw in his hand.

Wiranto did not follow Downer's script. His group was working to a different logic – the logic of exemplary mass punishment. The rest of Indonesia had to see that any province's decision to secede came at an awful price to its people. Also, just possibly, the scorched-earth policy might have finally goaded Fretilin military forces out of their UN cantonments into resumed fighting, giving a pretext for TNI to come back in force and annul the vote outcome on the basis that a civil war emergency had broken out in East Timor which still remained under Indonesian sovereignty.

It was a very close-run thing. Fretilin soldiers were heroically stoic in the face of weeks of something approaching genocide against their people. The huge world media coverage of the tragic humanitarian emergency in East Timor influenced President Clinton to send decisive warnings to Jakarta on 10 and 11 September, and was the basis for the unanimous Security Council endorsement of INTERFET (for which Australian military planners had been waiting since 4 September) on 12 September. Habibie capitulated the same day, and the rest is history.

None of what Australia did in this dramatic and tragic year can credibly be described as appeasement. The really big questions are about the morality and the foreign policy consequences (in terms of a seriously damaged relationship with Indonesia, hitherto our most important security partner in Southeast Asia) of what we did in 1999.

The moral questions concern whether the end – a chance for independence for East Timor – justified the means – deaths and dislocated lives of huge numbers of East Timorese people on the way, who were never consulted as to whether they wished to pay such a huge price. Australia and the UN offered false promises of security to the East Timorese before and after the election, which we knew could almost certainly not be honoured. This seems to me important. Also, East Timorese lives may actually have been used as policy levers, in that it was the international media's intensive reporting of extreme brutality towards these people that, in the end, gave Clinton the domestic political leverage for decisive policy action against the interests and 'face' of a traditionally close strategic partner in Asia.

There is no evidence that East Timorese independence leaders were ever consulted by Australia or the UN on whether such a high-risk policy for their people should have been undertaken. These decisions were taken for them from above, by Australia and by senior UN officials.

Maybe the end did justify the means: maybe, after so many wasted East Timorese deaths over the previous 25 years, it was worth more Timorese deaths now to take advantage of the brief window of opportunity Habibie had opened up, finally to give East Timor a chance at independence, and hopefully to 'lance the boil' that was constantly nagging at Australian–Indonesian relations.

Maybe – but I find the thought of such a Machiavellian calculation by Australians who were not personally at risk morally disquieting. I'd feel happier if I knew that somewhere along the line, the game plan had somehow been shared with at least a few senior East Timorese independence leaders. There's no evidence to date that it was.

In terms of the possible accountability of some TNI leaders at the time for war crimes against humanity, we have to seriously consider this question – were Australian ministers and senior advisers accessories before the fact? – if we are to be able squarely to discuss accountability and reconciliation issues with East Timorese and Indonesians in future.

Or perhaps all this suggests too much intelligence and diplomatic skill on Downer's and DFAT's part? Maybe Downer and his senior officials just blundered and stumbled helplessly and naively through the events of 1999 (which seems to be Paul Kelly's and Greg Sheridan's preferred explanation)? Were they knaves, or merely fools?

These are complicated questions not amenable to simple or sloganistic answers. I tried to detail such arguments in testimony to the Senate Foreign Affairs and Defence Committee's hearing on East Timor on 10 April 2000, which is on public Hansard internet. So far, Downer has dismissed such policy critiques, with public references to 'fantastic accusations' not worth responding to. The new DFAT official history *East Timor in Transition 1997–2000: An Australian Policy Challenge* offers no answers to these nagging questions; indeed, through its detailed commentary and many passages of retrospective wisdom after the event, it re-emphasises their relevance.

Birmingham had 25,000 words at his disposal to take the public debate forward on such important issues. Instead, he beat the tired drum of DFAT appeasement since 1975; Dick Woolcott gets the blame again.

Tony Kevin

[*This letter was received too close to publication for John Birmingham to respond.*]

from Jamie Mackie

Australia's troubled relations with Indonesia over East Timor provide an appropriately topical and important subject for the second issue of *Quarterly Essay*, while John Birmingham's lively style and full-blooded approach in *Appeasing Jakarta* have probably ensured that it will be widely read and frequently quoted in our various anti-Indonesian camps. But I doubt that it will prove very persuasive to many readers who are not already predisposed to agree with him. The picture of Indonesia he gives comes close to being a caricature. And I find myself so much at odds with both his central argument and the reasoning behind it that I feel his essay falls a long way short of the high standard set by Robert Manne's fine piece on the Stolen Generation controversy as a contribution to the kind of intelligent, well-informed public debate we need on national issues of this sort.

That is a pity, for criticisms could well be directed at many aspects of our handling of the East Timor problem and our relations with Indonesia over the last thirty years. But they would have to be argued much better than this if they are to be taken seriously as a basis for more effective and defensible policies appropriate to the tricky, unpredictable phase of the bilateral relationship now looming ahead of us. Even though the East Timor 'pebble in the shoe' is unlikely to cause more than minor difficulties between us, other secessionist tendencies in West Irian, Aceh and elsewhere may prove to be an even bigger irritant. And the blame for having started it all could easily be turned against Australia for its part in the East Timor drama.

Birmingham puts some parts of his case perceptively and often seems to be striving to be even-handed on contentious matters. His comments on Keating and on Gough Whitlam's policies on East Timor in 1974–5 and Dick Woolcott's role there (e.g. pp. 31, 45, 52) seemed not unfair to me, except for the know-all phrases about the latter's 'ultimately flawed vision', and such like. It is useful to be reminded that Indonesia's armed forces 'have never posed a serious threat to Australia' and could not hope to do so in the foreseeable future (p. 65). Also that our security rests partly on a quirk of geography – 'though the borders of the two countries are so close, their actual population and production centres are far removed' – and on various strategic advantages, 'an advanced industrial base, strong social cohesion and relatively sophisticated defence forces', as well as the ANZUS alliance. And that:

> Keating's policy of Asian engagement was commendable, and his particular emphasis on repairing the link to Jakarta was faultless – from an aspirational point of view. The institutional architecture that he, Evans, Ali Alatas and Suharto put in place consisted of exactly the sort of ties that should exist between neighbouring states which want to work for each other's benefit rather than against each other's interests. (p. 69)

But Birmingham then jumps in with another know-all remark that Keating was 'entirely wrong in thinking it was sustainable'. His policy was constructed on 'a foundation of ash and bones'. This is being wise after the event in the extreme. Could Birmingham or anyone else really have foreseen any of that five years before Suharto's fall? He is far too sweeping in his over-confident and far too unqualified assertions that 'the flaw at the heart of the New Order was its irreducible corruption and barbarism' and that because of the 'persistence of an informal power structure based on the remains of the New Order … the decaying but animated corpse of the old system is abroad in the land' and may have the best prospects of gaining control there. He may or may not be right about that last sentence, but a more tentative, sceptical tone would be more appropriate on all these analytical and evaluative issues rather than the purple prose, or gonzo journalism, he so often resorts to. ('Argument weak here – shout loudly' was a well-worn ploy of old-time public speakers.) None of us can peer into the cloudy mists of Indonesia's future with such self-confidence and certainty that we have it right.

The essay consists of two distinct parts, loosely interspersed. The first is the story-telling part which often makes a powerful appeal to the heart and is at times very moving, despite being written with what Peter Craven aptly calls a 'swashbuckling power of despatch' – or because of it, according to your taste. The stories he tells certainly cannot be gainsaid, even by those of us who might wish they could be. The behaviour of Indonesian troops in East Timor and the policies of the Jakarta government over its incorporation in both 1974–6 and ever since have often been appalling and indefensible. What Australia can or should do about it, however, is a far more complex question than Birmingham's pat suggestions imply.[i] The second part of the essay revolves around the author's starkly black-and-white theory about a 'systemic failure of analysis' and a 'dysfunctional paradigm' embraced by successive Australian governments for managing the relationship with our northern neighbour since 1974. Because any such theory must appeal to the head as well as the heart I find it much less cogent than the first part. But the questions it raises are important ones, so I want to focus mainly on that aspect of the essay, most of which has been aired many times over the last 30 years, but rarely with this sort of panache and self-assurance.

His interpretation of our policy errors in terms of the 'dysfunctional paradigm' strikes me as grossly over-simplified and reductionist. There are some grains of truth in it; but to attribute all those errors to just one such paradigm or mind-set in both the 1974–6 crisis and the 1990s is absurd. Many other factors were involved and the motivations of the key players in the drama (on all sides) differed radically in the two periods, as did the political situations confronting them. In neither case can the reasons behind our policies be boiled down simply to that easy catchword 'appeasement'. The reasons why Australia went along with Indonesian policies on Timor in 1974–6 were not at all the same as the reasons why we avoided 'standing up to' Jakarta more strongly after the Santa Cruz massacre of 1991 – and when we finally stood up to her bluntly in September 1999, we did so with even more far-reaching consequences (in terms of losing friends and alienating people) than we had intended. So can we perhaps infer that the 'paradigm' was no longer exerting its sinister influence by that time?

Was it 'appeasement'? What should (or could) Australia have done?

In the generally prevailing 1930s usage of that term, when the appeasers in Britain and France wanted to mollify Hitler with concessions in order to avoid war, the basic weakness of their strategy (quite apart from the moral overtones of the argument – and the implication of a lack of courage to resist him, so easy for armchair critics to throw at their opponents) was that essentially Hitler wanted and needed war, not just minor territorial concessions. Suharto, on the other hand, clearly did not want war, if he could avoid it. Hitler was a dangerous megalomaniac, rearming Germany relentlessly and addicted to diplomatic brinkmanship and bluffing. Suharto was a very cautious leader, by no means irrational or impervious to reason – not at all the picture one gets here from dismissive phrases about his 'ultimate lack of legitimacy' and far-reaching 'state terror'. He would certainly have preferred to avoid sending his troops in to accomplish the incorporation of East Timor, if he could achieve it through political means; but he had little alternative by the end of 1975.[ii] ('The old man ... did not want to carry the blame for the rest of his life for the invasion of East Timor,' said General Murdani as late as October 1975.) The Whitlam government was strongly urging him to avoid the use of force but could not have prevented it unless it was prepared to send Australian troops into East Timor, at a probable cost of escalating conflict with Indonesia, which was quite impossible to contemplate in 1975 for the most basic logistical reasons alone – our forces were quite inadequate even for a limited Timor operation – apart from many others.

In the 1990s, our only hope of applying greater pressure on Jakarta to change its policies on East Timor (beyond the quiet diplomatic representations our ministers and diplomats were constantly making) would have been to mobilise substantial international backing for our policies, such as we eventually managed to achieve in September 1999, almost miraculously, after the referendum on independence and the massacres that followed. Until then there was no chance that any of the great powers or the ASEAN states would support us over what they saw as simply a messy but minor decolonisation issue that was utterly peripheral to the former and too hot to handle for the latter. (In 1999 it came to be seen very differently there; and that was what made our intervention possible.) But Australia alone did not have sufficient political or economic clout – and today still does not – to exert more than marginal leverage on such matters, either in 1974–5 or in the 1990s. Hence it would have been quixotic in the extreme for a country in our position to get itself into a hostile wrangle with Jakarta over East Timor in either phase by resorting to would-be tougher policies which could not have achieved the goal of self-determination or independence there but would almost certainly have led to escalating conflict with Indonesia – to a point where our regional standing would have been badly damaged by Jakarta's inevitable antagonism to us.

If the charge of 'appeasing Jakarta' were watered down to the less dramatic proposition that 'We should have stood up to the Indonesians more strongly,' which I would have to accept as at least an arguable case (although rarely a compelling one), it would not have the same ring of instant persuasiveness. And it would need to be elaborated further in terms of what we should have done, and what the chances of success might have been if stronger measures to resist Indonesia's policies had been adopted. In 1974–5, some voices were raised by Australian diplomats and officials against the policy of working with rather than against the Indonesians over East Timor, as Birmingham notes; and in retrospect we can now see that they may have been right. The policies we were then pursuing failed utterly to achieve the twin objectives of self-determination and avoidance of the use of armed force which we were proclaiming. And a quarter-century later Indonesia's incorporation of East Timor had also proved a disastrous failure. The argument against 'unviable mini-states' on our northwestern border no longer carries the same weight as it did then. East Timor exists and we must help to make it survive. But the question of what we could then have done remains contentious.

It may sometimes be the most honourable path to espouse a quixotic cause even when the hopes of success are only slight, regardless of the political costs involved, where the choice is clearcut. That was not the case in 1975. Support for East Timor's independence may have been a more noble course to press vigorously in the appropriate UN committees, or similar bodies (but which?) in the hope of mobilising international pressure against Jakarta's incorporation strategy. But we would have support only from a tiny handful of African and minor communist-bloc countries, not from any of the major powers (not even from China) or the ASEAN or other Asian nations. It would have been no more than an empty gesture, achieving nothing, although at a cost of intense suspicion and hostility in Indonesia.[iii] It would almost certainly have undermined our one means of exercising some degree of influence and restraint in Jakarta by way of Gough Whitlam's carefully cultivated personal relationship with President Suharto. We couldn't have it both ways. The promise Suharto gave Whitlam at their Townsville meeting to avoid the use of force in pursuit of the goal of incorporation of East Timor was our one effective political lever, for he was reluctant to break it. We could not have achieved much more than that unless we had been able to persuade him that an outcome less than the incorporation of East Timor into Indonesian territory might have been feasible from his viewpoint. Opinions on the chances of doing that varied greatly, then and since, but it still remains an open question.

Since the late 1980s the main reason for Australia's reluctance to take a stronger stand against Indonesia over her human rights record in either East Timor or elsewhere in the archipelago has been a very different one. If we had got ourselves into an antagonistic situation with her over such matters, we would have had to pay a very high price on other fronts, especially in the damage to our capacity to become more closely engaged with her ASEAN neighbours and the rest of East Asia, which was rapidly becoming an economically dynamic region and one of our primary foreign policy concerns at a time of dramatic changes there. In that respect, Indonesia's co-operation with us in getting APEC off the ground (and in several other important international initiatives) was crucially important. But that is another story.

What sort of policy now?

Birmingham's scattered comments on what Australia's policies towards Indonesia should be in the future, if adopted, would propel us in an utterly disastrous direction, towards a minimalist and cold-hearted relationship with her instead of a potentially constructive one. (My own ideas on the direction we should be heading will be summarised briefly at the end of this piece.) He also ignores the fact that we are no longer dealing with the strong, over-centralised, highly personalistic regime of Suharto which exercised very tight control over foreign policy, but with the weak party-based governments and a far more pluralistic power structure which have emerged since 1998, as his comments below reveal:

> ... a fatal flaw lies at the heart of any state-to-state relationship that attempts to move beyond merely practical shared concerns.

> Attempting to re-establish a close connection with the very same forces that brought Indonesia to calamity and would do so again is not a very realistic prescription ...

> ... if we treat with a violent, repressive oligarchy, there will come a reckoning at some future point.

> ... as long as Indonesia remains an unstable and potentially authoritarian state, elemental political differences will inevitably preclude a close and abiding relationship.

It is utterly naive to imagine that Australia must wait until Indonesia ceases to be a 'potentially authoritarian state' – she may remain 'potentially' so for decades to come – before we try again to establish close relations with her, or that we can hope to be dealing with something other than the current elite or 'oligarchy' (violent, repressive or otherwise, which are matters we will simply have to accept, regardless of our distaste for it). In that case we could be waiting a long, long time; and we would have to pay a high price for our caution, or high moral principles, in terms of political and economic opportunities missed. We simply cannot afford to let 'elemental political differences' between the two countries or divergent values hold us back from trying to strengthen relations on both the official plane and the people-to-people level.[iv] That too would keep us waiting indefinitely, for Indonesia is not likely to adopt our values or political institutions in the foreseeable future, nor become the kind of 'benign, multicultural, free market democracy' Birmingham seems to envisage.

Unless our relations with Indonesia improve from the low point to which they plunged in September 1999 they are likely to deteriorate further, as mutual suspicions become deeper in both countries. Either they get better or they will get worse. If the latter, two disastrous consequences will follow. One is that siege mentalities are likely to develop in both countries, with inward-looking attitudes and racial prejudices increasing here while scapegoat-seeking attitudes over issues like West Irian will intensify there. The consequences could be disastrous. The other has to do with the broader regional dimension. Our relations with the rest of ASEAN and the Asian countries beyond are likely to suffer badly as long as we are at odds with Indonesia. She matters far more to them than we do.

A few words must be added on that all-important regional dimension, since it is utterly ignored by Birmingham. The main reason why Indonesia matters so much to Australia has less to do with the various ingredients of our bilateral relationship, important though some of them are, but with its implications for our much broader post-1945 drive to become integrated into the politics and economics of the entire East Asian region as a fully-fledged member, not as an outsider looking in, a 'white' nation surrounded by so many non-whites.[v] Unless we can achieve that in the decades ahead, our future prospects in this part of the world could be very bleak. And Indonesia is crucial to that process, not just because she could apply the sort of veto that Mahathir has been wielding recently against our efforts to become accepted as a member of the club (although that alone would be very serious for us, especially if we are at odds with her), but because, as one of the pioneering analysts of Australia's relations with her Asian neighbours, Macmahon Ball, put it many years ago,

> If Australia cannot manage to maintain good relations with Indonesia, we will have little hope of building up any kind of worthwhile relationship with the rest of our region.

That doesn't mean we must always pander to Jakarta (we don't), or avoid opposing her on issues of importance to us. We did so during the Konfrontasi conflict of 1963–6 and the earlier West Irian dispute, to a point where Australian and Indonesian troops were shooting at each other on the Sarawak frontier at one stage. But the two governments handled those issues without being driven by adverse public opinion to any serious rupture of diplomatic relations. We can no doubt do so again if necessary. The deeper point, however, must be to recognise that our policies towards Jakarta should always be interlinked with our broader policies towards the entire East Asian international system.

Birmingham writes that 'wishful thinking is no substitute for cold realism' and that 'a truly hard-headed approach' is needed. No one in his right mind would dispute such worthy platitudes. But what he means by these words is in fact highly problematic. Such an approach, he goes on, must not ignore the fact that democracy in Indonesia 'is a weak endangered concept with only a few genuine supporters among the ruling elites' (a contentious assessment) and that it must always take account of the question: 'what is sustainable over the very long term?' But how long does that mean – five years, or ten, or until events make it irrelevant? And who can tell us confidently how to answer any of those questions? Or whether democracy currently has few 'genuine' supporters among the elites or many, or whether our policy towards Indonesia over the next few years should depend heavily on the answers to them? These are vastly more tangled issues than he seems to realise.

What, then, should be the main features of our future policies towards Indonesia? I will simply offer a few bald suggestions, although they all need much fuller elaboration.

- We must above all ensure that our policies towards Indonesia and our overall bilateral relationship with her are not out of kilter with our broader regional relations with the other ASEAN and East Asian nations, which must be governed primarily by our national interests in the wider East Asian international power balance, on three planes, strategic, economic and political. We cannot let those primary foreign policy objectives be subordinated to our sense of outrage about what is happening in East Timor, West Irian or Aceh, or any other part of the archipelago – not even by breaches of human rights there, unless the rest of ASEAN and Japan are prepared to back us, as they were in September 1999. That does not mean we should neglect human rights issues, but they cannot be elevated to such prominence that they become the tail that wags the dog.
- The maintenance of a unified Indonesia is very much in Australia's national interest (although preferably a much more decentralised one) and must

remain a primary goal of our policies towards her. The political complexities of dealing with a badly fissured archipelago made up of mini-states could prove horrific for Australia. But maintaining a viable balance between that goal and our commitments to the preservation of human rights and inter-ethnic harmony in the troubled areas will always be a very tricky matter of political judgement, depending on well-informed knowledge of local circumstances, not just on abstract principles.

- The general character of our relationship with her should be restored to something much closer to the Keating–Evans policies of the early 1990s (as summarised above by Birmingham) than to John Howard's boastful 'regional sheriff' rhetoric of 1999. But we should avoid ever again being manoeuvred into the kind of close reliance on personalised relationships to a single leader in Jakarta that Keating established with Suharto (unavoidable, no doubt, at that time, but no longer necessary) or intimate involvement with the military (see below). Instead we should put much greater emphasis on building up strong people-to-people and institutional ties rather than just official relationships.

- A corollary to this must be for our embassy officials to build up the widest possible diversity of contacts with all the main political actors on the Indonesian stage, not just with senior ministers and bureaucrats. In an increasingly pluralistic and democratising polity that should be much easier in future. Suharto's one-man domination of key decision-making processes was *sui generis*, and fortunately not likely to recur in the near future.

- The Keating rhetoric that 'no country matters to Australia as much as Indonesia' should be modified towards Howard's version that she is 'one of the most important'. While the wording may seem a trivial matter, the expectations generated are not.

- What about the military? That will always be a difficult question requiring delicate and well-informed judgement, for we cannot just turn our backs on it in disgust, or disregard its continuing importance in Indonesia's political system (although far less than previously) or its role as the key upholder of the country's national unity and integrity.

- It should not be imagined that we can avoid official dealings with former elements of the New Order power structure, such as Golkar or the military. They are likely to remain on the political scene there for a long time and it's for Indonesians themselves to get rid of them, not us. There are many admirably reformist and progressive groups in Indonesia who deserve whatever help we or other outsiders can give to them in such matters, rather than to their enemies. But this is a tricky path to tread, for it can easily give rise to angry accusations of outside interference in Indonesia's sovereign realm of domestic affairs.

- Finally, it must never be forgotten that there are limits to the extent to which any part of our foreign policies, in Indonesia or elsewhere, can be pursued in the face of hostile public opinion within Australia, as Birmingham rightly observes. (On the other hand, our foreign policies should never again be permitted to become as poll-driven or Hanson-conscious as they have been under Howard and Downer.) Birmingham is also right in urging that: 'No administration in Jakarta should ever again be allowed to assume it will have Australian support when it turns the machinery of oppression on its own people.

Jamie Mackie

---

[i] The complexity of the issues confronting Australian officials in 1974–5 is abundantly revealed in the official DFAT collection of documents on *Australia and the Indonesian Incorporation of East Timor, 1974–76. Documents on Australian Foreign Policy*, edited by Wendy Way; Melbourne University Press, 2000. In a review article on this I have given my own assessment of the options open to us then in the *Australian Journal of International Affairs*, vol. 55 (1): 133–43. See also the useful piece by James Cotton in the same issue,' "Part of the Indonesian World": Lessons in East Timor policy-making, 1974–6', ibid., pp. 119–132.

[ii] Hindsight can blind us to the important historical fact that Suharto had nothing like such dominance of the Jakarta power structure in 1974–5 as he achieved in later years (because of the crippling Pertamina debt crisis and the Malari riots of early 1974), so he must have realised that if he failed to bring about the incorporation of East Timor after setting it as his preferred outcome his hold on the presidency could have become extremely precarious. Many old-time nationalists were already complaining in those years that he was not a real nationalist like his predecessor, Sukarno, who would never have allowed Indonesia to be pushed around by such political midgets as Portugal or its Fretilin protégé.

[iii] It is not widely recognized in Australia that there was a great deal of suspicion in Indonesia in 1974–5 that our motive for opposing Indonesia's aim of incorporating East Timor was that we must have our own nefarious plans to acquire the former

colony ourselves as a bastion against her. In view of the prevalence of conspiracy theories there, that suspicion could easily have been fanned into blazing hostility.

iv At the unofficial level of people-to-people relations or institutional and economic relations of the kind Birmingham applauded as part of the Keating–Evans policy, remarkably impressive progress is in fact still being made despite the top-level tensions intruding since 1999. Hundreds of Indonesians, including ministers and generals, are now sending their children to school or university in Australia and hundreds of Australians are now working in Indonesia, a far cry from ten years ago. This is crucially important in 'putting ballast into the relationship' so that it will not again be overturned by sudden political squalls.

v There is a racial (and frequently racist) aspect of Australia's broader relationship with all our Asian neighbours that we must try to change by every means possible over the next century. They as well as we need to get away from those hoary old binary stereotypes about 'Europe–Asia', 'us–them', 'white–black' and so on – and persuade Asians to get beyond them too. So long as they linger on in our minds, and so long as Australia is still associated in Asia with the old racist attitudes that sustained the White Australia Policy against them, our steady progress towards becoming one of the most multiracial and multicultural countries in this part of the world cannot make the impact it should; so we will remain 'the odd man out, looking in' instead of being accepted inside the club as not essentially different from them, which we are still thought to be, and still think ourselves to be.

APPEASING JAKARTA | *Correspondence*

from Paul Monk

John Birmingham's essay *Appeasing Jakarta: Australia's Complicity in the East Timor Tragedy* is marred by what seems to be very poor drafting. It reads as though the author had scanned a hastily assembled batch of available materials and then dashed off his polemic. From someone who is presented to us as 'the most notable "new journalist" we have', it is a poor showing. If this is, as Peter Craven remarks, 'an essay written in flowing colours with a strong narrative streak and a swashbuckling power of dispatch', one can only say that the colours flow into one another a bit, the narrative streaks away with itself and the swash makes the argument buckle.

Right from the outset, Birmingham jumps around between 1975 and 1999 in a manner which leaves the informed reader quite unclear what precise point he intends to make. Unhappily, he nowhere corrects this tendency. He leaps backward and forward between 1975 and 1999, 1974 and 1991, 1974 and 1975 in a way which disorganises his implicit argument. His grasp of the precise sequence of events often seems to be hazy. He has occasional insights, but they are not presented systematically. Indeed, he appears quite uncertain himself about what his insights really are. For instance, he vacillates repeatedly between morally rebuking the Australian government and statements that its fault was *not* moral, but analytical.

Consider the following, from page 3, as an example of his manner of writing:

It was assumed before the invasion in 1975 that the East Timorese would accept incorporation. When they resisted, involving Jakarta in a long and brutal counterinsurgency campaign, genuine power realists should have foreseen the ultimately futile and self-destructive endgame which would play itself out there. But other more significant Australian policy makers, many of whom prided themselves on the 'hard-headed realism' of their analysis and approach, deluded themselves. They chose to ignore dissonant information and analysis from within their own bureaucracy, preferring instead the consolations of wishful thinking. Foremost among their number are Gough Whitlam and Richard Woolcott.

The sentiments expressed here may be such that many readers glide over the passage without noticing any particular problem with it. This is especially likely to be so if they have no detailed knowledge of the matters to which Birmingham is referring. Consider, however, the way it looks if you parse it a bit more carefully.

First, it was not, in fact, assumed 'before the invasion in [December] 1975' that the East Timorese would accept incorporation. This assumption had been jettisoned by many top figures in Canberra in December 1974. Birmingham actually knows this, because he points it out further on in his essay. Why then state here that it was so assumed in 1975? Second, the reference to a 'long and brutal counter-insurgency campaign' suggests a perspective extending for some years after 1975, but how is this supposed to bear on judgements made 'before the invasion'? Third, he asserts that 'genuine power realists' should have 'foreseen' – once the campaign had become long and brutal – how it would end. Perhaps, but this is not self-evident. Many insurgencies have been crushed in history.

Fourth, he then remarks that 'other more significant policy makers...deluded themselves.' Other than whom? He hasn't mentioned anyone. In any case, if these shadowy individuals were not very significant, what difference would it have made if they had foreseen how things would end? Fifth, he then states that chief among these others were Gough Whitlam and Richard Woolcott. But Gough Whitlam was out of office by the time the (overt) invasion began in 1975. In short, in this particular passage, Birmingham is jumping all over the place, his heart pounding but his intellectual craftsmanship floundering.

Unfortunately, this is far from being the only example of such flawed craftsmanship. Consider his statement, on page 4, that Australia's 'official position' in 1974 was 'based on profound ignorance and the uninformed personal preferences of Prime Minister Whitlam'. This is simply untrue. The documentary record makes it abundantly clear that Australia's official position was based not on profound ignorance at all, but on explicit and frequent briefings by Indonesian insiders and sound intelligence from the field in Timor. Nor was Whitlam 'uninformed'. He was very closely briefed. The problem was that he chose to ignore his briefing notes and tell Suharto that he personally believed East Timor should be part of Indonesia. Although this was not then Australian policy – read Australia's official position – he told Suharto, it soon would be, because he, the great Gough, would make it so.

Especially topsy-turvy is Birmingham's treatment of the moral versus realist issue in the making of Australia's policy. On page 2, he states that 'Abandonment, betrayal, ineptitude and moral cowardice' characterised Australia's policy. Then, on page 5, he declares, 'The failure of our foreign policy elite was not ethical but intellectual.' On page 55, he denounces what he calls the 'amoral sophistry embraced by Foreign Affairs' and on page 56 he goes so far as to rebuke what he calls 'our cowardice and our gross moral turpitude'. Yet on page 64 he states that the real failure of the 'hard heads and realists', in both 1975 and 1999, was not moral. It was that they espoused a policy 'wedded to desire and not cold calculation'.

He never sorts this out, with the consequence that the reader has to wonder whether he believes that 'cold calculation' and moral reason naturally go together, or that the former must, in foreign policy, be given greater weight than the latter. Richard Woolcott has, of course, been widely vilified for arguing the second of these propositions in his cables of 1975. If Birmingham believes Woolcott erred only in being insufficiently cold and realistic, why does he speak of 'amoral sophistry' and 'moral turpitude'? If he believes that Woolcott and others were morally at fault, why does he state that 'cold calculation' must be the criterion of foreign policy?

Birmingham plainly needs a more nuanced understanding of the dilemmas involved in foreign policy making. His failure to think through what he is arguing suggests that he might, in a crisis, prove quite as amoral as any of the diplomats he is criticising. Suppose cold calculation dictated, in a readily imaginable scenario, that it *was* in the national interest that large numbers of people be abandoned to a brutal fate. Would Birmingham then simply recommend 'cold calculation'? His remarks about Woolcott suggest that he would – and would expect others to. Woolcott's offence, he asserts, was simply to have miscalculated. But how, ultimately, under the pressure of circumstances, are statesmen or diplomats to be certain in such matters?

A further example of a confused judgement, which seems to have been written in haste and not revised, is Birmingham's statement, on page 30, that 'East Timor was the prism through which everything else was viewed' by both Canberra and Jakarta from 1975 until at least 1999. This is, surely, precisely the reverse of the truth, at least as far as Australian policy is concerned. East Timor was consistently viewed from Canberra through the prism of the priority placed on cordial and stable relations with Jakarta. In Jakarta, it was viewed through a different prism: that of an overweening nationalism distorted – as many a nationalism has been – by the ambitions of elite circles of military and intelligence officers.

That Birmingham has not spent sufficient time analysing the documentary record is indicated by his summary judgement, on page 55, that, 'The repetitive restatement of Whitlam's view that good relations with Jakarta came first, and that East Timor would be better off opting for Indonesian rule by genuine vote had placed a deep fracture in the centre of Australian strategy *which was never resolved.*' [my italics] It *was* resolved, however: first by the expedient urged in 1975 by Richard Woolcott, of dropping the 'genuine vote' idea and acknowledging Indonesian incorporation of East Timor; then, in 1999, by reversing this policy and supporting the genuine vote after all. The problem was not that the fracture was 'never resolved'. The problem was that the Indonesians simply could not subdue tenacious resistance to their incorporation of East Timor.

Nowhere in his essay does Birmingham venture to suggest what he would have done in Woolcott's position, as ambassador, in 1975–76. Having inherited Whitlam's unworkable policy, the Ambassador had to provide counsel – with Whitlam still in office until late 1975 – as to which way to move to resolve the 'fracture' to which he himself explicitly drew attention. Addressing this question requires the sort of attention to detail and the sequence of events which Birmingham does not seem to have the patience for. What may have been possible in 1974 was not necessarily possible by the time Woolcott became ambassador, much less in late 1975.

Perhaps the most interesting aspect of Birmingham's essay is his attempt to adumbrate a theory of cognitive dysfunction in policy and intelligence bureaucracies. Drawing on a recent article by Bill Maley about the making of policy in 1999, he summarises 'four systemic problems' within DFAT: obsession with the 'big picture' becoming 'a rationale for wishing away uncomfortable realities'; a rigid hierarchy which severely discourages the questioning of established 'orthodoxies'; an entrancement with 'the mystique of its own communiques' as compared with 'competing sources of information'; and the tendency to muddle through rather than 'engage in contingency planning'.

He has a point about DFAT. It is a far from perfect organisation. The phenomena referred to by Maley certainly occur, with varying degrees of intensity. Yet by Birmingham's own account, there were 'hundreds' of people who, in 1974–75 and later did challenge orthodoxies and call for alternatives. The problem was not entirely one of what he calls 'cluelessness and denial', least of all in 1974–75, when the record plainly shows much debate and dissent. It was, rather, that the *executive* – rather than the bureaucracy – exerted strong leadership in a direction which turned out to entail consequences that intelligence officers and diplomats *did* foresee and to which they often *did* draw attention.

Birmingham writes of how 'formal hierarchies such as the military or diplomatic corps' can suffer from cognitive pathologies. He is correct in this. They can and often they do. Unfortunately, he does not offer any suggestions as to how one can have military and diplomatic organisations which will not suffer from such pathologies. Norman Dixon, in his famous book *The Psychology of Military Incompetence*, suggested that the problem, at least in the British military, needed to be overcome by better potty training, so that one ended up with less anal retentive officers. This has understandably provoked scepticism and even laughter since it was written. But Birmingham does not even offer us a *potty* idea.

Though such organisations may serve a liberal and democratic society, he observes, they are not themselves liberal or democratic. True enough. Does he then argue that they should or can be? Not really. He does seem to believe that they, or the executive, need to be more responsive to public opinion, but he does not enlarge on how precisely this is to be institutionally arranged. While he seems to endorse Bill Maley's call for better cognitive practices in the bureaucracy, he doesn't take any time at all to reflect on exactly how this might be organised. Nor does he reflect at all on relations between the 'formal hierarchies' and Cabinet, even though it seems to have been *there*, if anywhere, that the system malfunctioned most clearly, in both 1974–75 and 1998–99.

Finally, as he looks to the future, apart from recommending that an ill-defined 'cold realism' replace 'wishful thinking', Birmingham declares gloomily, on page 29, that 'the unavoidable marginalisation of Australia's tiny economy will erode what little leverage it can apply to international affairs.' Exactly how this should affect the institutional approach we take to making foreign policy he does not venture to suggest. The statement itself, however, is strangely at odds with his observation, on page 75, that even prior to the crash of 1997, 'the Australian economy was twice the size of Indonesia's, despite being based on a population roughly one tenth the size.'

All these remarks might be taken to suggest that I disagree with Birmingham's basic outlook on the history of Australian East Timor policy. I don't, actually. I think he has more or less got the picture. The problem is that he has got the picture blurred and this is a disservice to anyone reading his essay who is not well informed and alert. Those who are, on the other hand, have no need to read it at all.

The budding novelist, the author of *He Died with a Felafel in His Hand*, wanted to be expressed on this vexed subject. The result, regrettably, does not pass muster as a useful contribution to the literature. Perhaps, though, he deserves some credit for the fact that at least he tried. One might say, a little facetiously, *He Tried with a Farrago in His Hand*.

Paul Monk

John Birmingham

As I read Frank Brennan's letter, my mortal sin as well as Robert Manne's is that neither of us are insiders. I stand guilty as charged and await my fate before God. If Robert will forgive me replying on his behalf, however, I might point out that his essay was not simply concerned with the stolen generations as such, but rather with the denial of their existence by a loose cabal of newspaper columnists. As Manne has been writing on this topic for many years, and engaging in debate with those very columnists, I fail to see why he cannot be considered an insider.

Brennan seems to be labouring under the delusion that there are legions of insiders straining at the leash to unburden themselves of secrets they have kept from us for decades. While I agree it would be a marvellous thing if they gave it up for the public, I won't be holding my breath for that happy day. Insiders do tell their own stories occasionally, but they are almost inevitably pleas for understanding, rather than confessions. Former US Secretary of Defense Robert MacNamara's Vietnam epiphany is the exception that proves the rule. Perhaps if Brennan is serious about this point he could chance his arm in the business, set up a little publishing venture, something like Mea Culpa Books, and throw open his doors to the sinful.

But I am being a little harsh. Brennan would have preferred to hear more of the voices of the East Timorese and I can't fault him for that. But I was not telling their story, I was telling ours, and where they do appear it is not as central players but as pawns. That is the sad reality of East Timor's history, and a few more quotes here and there would not have changed it.

The issue of insiders and outsiders runs through much of this correspondence, although often as subtext. Monk and Mackie in particular seem aggrieved by the intrusion of an outsider into what was previously the very cosy preserve of experts. (And how well those experts have served us over the years.) Neither seems to have grasped the basic fact that these essays are not written for players and insiders. They are meant for a general audience that probably would not engage with such issues in the normal course of events. Each writer will no doubt deal with this in their own way, but for me it meant initially emphasizing narrative over discursive text and bringing whatever descriptive powers I might have to the task of making the reader understand what it is like to run before the guns. This is almost unheard of in academic writing – and partly why our academics' published efforts are so widely ignored. I cannot help but feel that Mackie and Monk have somehow taken offence at what they would consider to be gross showmanship.

Too bad.

Returning to my opening comments, some readers will be surprised that given the robust and sometimes stinging nature of both Campbell's and Aarons's letters, I have little problem with their critique. I can accept without reservation Aaron's argument that there is a large vacuum in the essay occupying the spot where an attack on the Fraser government's handling of the issue should rightly be found. I was aware of that fault even as I wrote the essay, but became so engaged in the task of comparing 1974–5 and 1999 that I decided to leave Fraser's record for others to consider. *Appeasing Jakarta* was not meant to be a definitive and exhaustive account, and so I felt reasonably comfortable with that decision. I am even more comfortable and – dare I say it – relaxed, now that Aarons has devoted his valuable time to rectifying my own tardiness.

Campbell, of course, is a true insider and brings that perspective to his argument. Again, I am happy to take my lumps from him. His correspondence is of great value in fleshing out some points that I raced over. I am sorry that he seems to have misinterpreted one or two lines of argument in the essay; for instance, presuming that I am promoting a pro-Defence line over Foreign Affairs. That was not my intention, and had I had more time and space I would have spent it, not on the Fraser years as Aarons would have liked, but on the 'truly myopic zeal' of Defence for its relationship with the Indonesian armed forces in later years of the Hawke–Keating administrations. That Campbell has read this misinterpretation into the essay is undoubtedly my fault rather than his. In mitigation of another censure, that the essay is of little help in formulating future policy, I must declare that such was never my intention and so I feel a little put out to be so indicted.

I must also thank Jamie Mackie for the considerable time and effort he has obviously given to his reply. Naturally I do not agree with many of his points, but apart from occasionally succumbing to the urge to criticise the author rather the argument, Mackie mostly presents a fair example of reasoned commentary.

Even if he is wrong. For instance, he thinks that accusing Keating of erecting a security architecture on a foundation of ashes and bone is 'being wise after the event'. As indeed it is. But that is a privilege enjoyed by all commentators and analysts reviewing historical material. It also goes without saying that not all critics of Keating's treaty spoke in retrospect. There were many voices raised against it from the first. I suppose, however, that not many of them would have been heard amongst Mackie's peer network – given that in September 1999 the *Sydney Morning Herald* described him as a proud and long-time member of a pro-Indonesian policy 'mafia' – a crucial identifying detail which somehow went missing from his reply.

One of Mackie's principal objections to the essay is to the thesis that a paradigm, in other words a way of thinking, exerted a malign influence over Australian policy towards Indonesia for 25 years. It would be fair to say that of all the negative reactions to *Appeasing Jakarta*, both published and unpublished, this particular point seems to inspire the most willing response. This is understandable, given that the respondents and their mouthpieces are standing naked before history, looking for a fig leaf to hide their embarrassment. Perhaps we should look again at Donald Watt's modern definition of the word appeasement – 'purchasing peace for one's own interests by sacrificing the interests of others'. Divorced of its odious 1930s connotations – which I note Mackie simply cannot help but resort to – Watt's definition seems to me to be a remarkably concise synopsis of the paradigm, or world view, which informed Australian policy from 1974 to the present day. In fact, it still seems to inform Mackie's opinions today.

There are many Australian intelligence officers and police officers who have returned from East Timor who would argue that it still holds sway amongst significant players in Canberra. So no, Professor Mackie, we cannot perhaps infer that the 'paradigm' no longer exerts 'its sinister influence'. If you doubt the truth of that, I'm sure Captain Andrew Plunkett or former AFP officer Wayne Sievers would be happy to give you the benefit of their practical experience in this matter. Who knows? Perhaps a little time spent away from the 'pro-Jakarta policy mafia' might even be good for the soul. Just as spending a couple of days detained in a *Kopassus* torture chamber at the pleasure of General Prabowo Subianto might give you pause to wonder whether my characterisation of the New Order regime as a brutal dictatorship had more than a grain of truth in it. There are hundreds of thousands, if not millions, of Suharto's victims who would probably be glad of the opportunity to debate the point with you, were they alive.

Mackie seems to think that I am promoting a confrontational policy towards Jakarta, that I supported some 'quixotic' headlong rush to conflict in 1975. He can only infer all this, however; I never made such a preposterous suggestion. To attribute it to me is a skilful rhetorical device – a good deal more sophisticated than his rather facile attempt to insinuate that I was comparing the New Order with the Nazi regime – but it is just a device. If Mackie and his colleague Monk really must know what I think Australia should have done in 1974-5, I'll tell them. We should have warned the Indonesians that they could not subdue the colony. We should have warned them that they could expect no support, only condemnation, from Australia. And we should have warned them that they were marching into their own Vietnam. Do I believe that this would have made a difference to the outcome? No. The history of East Timor would have been the same. But Australia's history would have been different in one crucial respect. We would not have shamed ourselves. I agree with Mackie that there would have been a political price to pay. I guess we part company on whether that price would have been worth it.

I do not accept Mackie's accusation that the essay utterly ignores the all-important regional dimension. I make exactly the same point he does when saying that Australia cannot afford the political consequences of prolonged and severe hostility towards Jakarta. I am not sure why Mackie chose to misrepresent me on this matter, because we are actually of one mind on it. Finally, in examining his prescription for the relationship, I find his ambivalent and evasive suggestion about any future dealings with the TNI to be characteristic of the overall flaws in his approach. He seems to agree that the Indonesian military is worthy of our disgust, but is unwilling to resile from treating with them.

Hunter S. Thompson once said something to the effect of: 'They'll beat you when you're wrong and they'll beat you when you're right. It just doesn't hurt as much when you're right.' In the case of a graceless oaf like Doctor Paul Monk, you'd have to clarify that rule slightly, because I doubt it would hurt very much even if you were wrong. Having perused his scatterbrained missive, I now understand what it's like to be attacked by a toothless tiger; the fleeting moment of panic as the brightly coloured and menacing beast lands on your chest, followed by confusion, mutating into giggles and finally uncontrolled gales of laughter at the soft, wet and not entirely unpleasant sensation of being ferociously gummed.

It is a temptation when presented with such a feeble, stricken piece of rhetoric to devote considerably more time to it than is warranted. And I am afraid, good reader, that you may think less of me because I find myself unable to resist that temptation. Such large, slow-moving targets as Monk are rare outside the bovine world, and when one is foolish enough to amble onto the killing floor of its own volition, natural selection demands that it be put down.

But where to begin? Perhaps with Monk's inability to follow a narrative. He seems to have been deeply troubled by the way *Appeasing Jakarta* was structured, saying that it 'leaps backward and forward between 1975 and 1999, 1974 and 1991, 1974 and 1975 in a way which disorganises the argument'. I must confess myself at a total loss as to how best to answer this point. In all of the responses, both positive and negative, I have received to the essay, nobody other than Monk raised this as a problem. I suppose this is unsurprising, given that many bright children often master the ability to follow a non-linear narrative from a comparatively early age. Sadly this skill seems to have entirely eluded the good doctor. I can only suggest that if the old Thinking Institute offers some basic remedial reading courses, he avail himself of a staff discount. Immediately. His confusion leads him to assume that I am befuddled as to whether the failure of first the Whitlam and then successive Australian governments was moral or analytic. I am sorry I could not dice that argument up into more bite-sized pieces, which Monk might then have been able to digest. But I thought that the core point of the essay was quite simple: that the original failure was analytic, and from that moral consequences flowed. To argue one does not negate the other. Monk attempts this at some length later on, in tandem with a completely gratuitous suggestion that I would prove as amoral in a similar situation as the diplomats I was criticising. I suppose, once upon a time, a gentleman would demand satisfaction at dawn for such a slur on his honour. I shall just have to make do with the hope that most people will see Monk's performance as the worthless posturing of a self-important blowhard.

Having confused himself, his target and his readers, Monk becomes entangled in a confused passage where he attempts to perform an autopsy on one particular paragraph in the hope that he might tease out some pathological fault in my argument. Unfortunately he achieves a quite spectacular series of self-inflicted wounds, in which he first accuses me of one thing and then provides my own defence in the next few lines. Bewildered? So was I. Perhaps two examples might suffice. I had written: 'It was assumed before the invasion in 1975 that the East Timorese would accept incorporation.' Monk says this is not the case, but it plainly was. The view was not universally held. Indeed I went to some length in the essay to demonstrate that no views were universally held about East Timor. But it is undeniable that some of the most important power players in the period before the invasion assumed the East Timorese would accept their lot. Whitlam said as much directly to Suharto.

In the same strand of argument, Monk asks who the policymakers are that I claim were suffering from self-delusion. I apparently do not name them. But I'd

like you to pay very close attention to this extract from Monk's reply (I have
snipped out one sentence, which I don't think affects the line of his argument,
but readers can make that decision for themselves by checking his original text):

> Fourth, he then remarks that other more significant policy makers
> ... deluded themselves. Other than whom? He hasn't mentioned
> anyone ... Fifth, he then states that chief among these others were
> Gough Whitlam and Richard Woolcott.

I think, given the above, I'll leave readers to make up their own minds about
whose argument is disordered. I will say, however, that it was at this point that
I began to feel genuine sympathy for any fee-paying students of the Thinking
Institute.

Monk's point – that I was wrong to claim our position in 1974 was based on
a profound ignorance of that situation in East Timor – flies in the face of the
statement in December 1974 by Michael Cook, First Assistant Secretary, North
and West Asia Division, that at the first meeting of Foreign Affairs division heads:

> No one knew much about Portuguese Timor. There seemed to have
> been a basic assumption that Portuguese Timor would be like West
> Irian; the people would accept integration, and from this assumption
> followed our commitment to an internationally acceptable act of self determination.

Monk's claim that East Timor was not the prism through which the Jakarta
relationship was viewed and distorted for 25 years would be news to Paul
Keating, who was obsessed with not holding the wider relationship to ransom
over the issue. Surely if East Timor was of no consequence, as Monk seems to
believe, there would have been no reason for the Keating Government to invest
so much political capital in trying to work around it.

A feeling of great weariness comes over me as I force my way through the rest
of the doctor's points. When he is not misinterpreting the most simple of statements, he indulges himself in a taste for the bizarre, such as his foray into the
potty training of the British officer corps. Am I supposed to reply to this?

On the evidence of this letter, it beggars belief that Monk could have risen
to the highest levels of academe anywhere other than an internet university
based on the edge of a Tijuana whorehouse district. But he is indeed closely
connected with a number of prestigious universities, where we must assume he
has demonstrated some flair or talent that is entirely absent from his incursion

into this debate. His irrational and contradictory arguments are embarrassing enough, but to allow him to compound the cringe with his egregiously unfunny attempts at wit was simply cruel. If any of his academic colleagues actually read his piece before it slithered under the door of my publisher, they should really have said something. It was wrong to allow the poor man to humiliate himself in such a public fashion.

John Birmingham

Mark Aarons is the author (with Robert Domm) of *East Timor: A Western Made Tragedy* and, most recently, *War Criminals Welcome*.

John Birmingham is the author of *Leviathan*, a history of Sydney, and *He Died with a Felafel in his Hand*. His essay *Appeasing Jakarta* was the second in the *Quarterly Essay* series.

Fr Frank Brennan SJ AO has written extensively on Aboriginal rights. He is the Director of Uniya, the Jesuit Social Justice Centre in Sydney. For the past year, he has been the Director of the Jesuit Refugee Service in East Timor. He is a board member of the Australian Studies Centre of the University of Indonesia.

Duncan Campbell is a former diplomat who was Minister in Australia's Mission to the UN in New York in 1975 responsible for decolonisation issues. He is a regular opinion contributor to the *Australian*.

Tony Kevin is visiting fellow at the Research School of Pacific and Asian Studies, ANU and former Australian Ambassador to Cambodia.

Jamie Mackie is former Emeritus Professor at ANU, and is currently attached to the Indonesia Project in the Research School of Pacific and Asian Studies, ANU.

Paul Monk is Senior Fellow at the Australian Thinking Skills Institute. He teaches security issues in contemporary Asia at Melbourne University's Institute of Asian Languages and Societies and intelligence and statecraft at the ANU's Graduate School of Public Policy.

Guy Rundle is the co-editor of *Arena* magazine, a magazine of political and social comment, and the writer of *Your Dreaming*, the latest political satire from Max Gillies. He is a regular essayist for the *Age* and the *Sydney Morning Herald* and columnist for the *Adelaide Review*.

www.ingramcontent.com/pod-product-compliance
Lightning Source LLC
Chambersburg PA
CBHW081648270326
41933CB00018B/3389